Moslems

Their beliefs, practices, and politics

ISBN 0-9661325-6-4

Moslems
Their beliefs, practices, and politics

GABRIEL OUSSANI
and
HILAIRE BELLOC

ROGER A. McCAFFREY
PUBLISHING

Box 1209 • Ridgefield, CT 06877

CONTENTS

PUBLISHER'S NOTE

September 11, 2001, saw the resurgence of a time-worn cliché: Our world is, most definitely, changed forever. What those who utter it may not realize is that "our world" is that which used to be called "Christian civilization."

While it may be true that Moslems come in many peaceful varieties, something about them as a group must have inspired Hilaire Belloc, the British Catholic historian and social commentator, to caution — in the 1930s — that Christian Europe was not done with them yet.

He could not even have imagined that "Moslem fundamentalists" would threaten the United States of America as well. And it would have been beyond impossible in his mind that both Europe and the U.S. would import them, and give them homes, in the millions.

This book is a collection of articles by Gabriel Oussani about Moslems — their origins, beliefs, politics and practices — published in the original *Catholic Encyclopedia* early in the 20th century. In addition, Belloc's prescient essay of 1936 is included.

Allah

The name of God in Arabic. It is a compound word from the article, *'al*, and *ilāh*, divinity, and signifies "the god" *par excellence*. This form of the divine name is in itself a sure proof that *ilāh* was at one time an appellative, common to all the local and tribal gods. Gradually, with the addition of the article, it was restricted to one of them who took precedence of the others; finally, with the triumph of monotheism, He was recognized as the only true God. In one form or another this Hebrew root occurs in all Semitic languages as a designation of the Divinity; but whether it was originally a proper name, pointing to a primitive monotheism, with subsequent deviation into polytheism and further rehabilitation, or was from the beginning an appellative which became a proper name only when the Semites had reached monotheism is a much debated question. It is certain, however, that before the time of Mohammed, owing to their contact with Jews and Christians, the Arabs were generally monotheists. The notion of Allah in Arabic theology is substantially the same as that of God among the Jews, and also among the Christians, with the exception of the Trinity, which is positively excluded in the Koran, cxii: "Say God, is one God, the eternal God, he begetteth not, neither is he begotten and there is not any one like unto him." His attributes denied by the heterodox Motazilites, are ninety-nine in number. Each one of them is represented by a bead in the Mussulmanic chaplet, while on the one hundredth and larger bead, the name of *Allah* itself is pronounced. It is preposterous to assert with Curtiss (*Ursemitische Religion*, 119) that the nomadic tribes of Arabia, consider seriously the *Oum-el-Gheith*, "mother of the rain", as the bride of Allah; and even if the expression were used, such symbolical language would not impair, in the least, the purity of monotheism held by those tribes. (Cf. *Revue Biblique*, Oct., 1906, 580 sqq.) Let it be noted that although Allah is an Arabic term, it is used by all Moslems, whatever be their language, as the name of God.

R. BUTIN

Nihil Obstat, March 1, 1907. Remy Lafort, S.T.D., Censor
Imprimatur. +John Cardinal Farley, Archbishop of New York

Mohammed and Mohammedanism

The Founder

Mohammed, "the Praised One", the prophet of Islam and the founder of Mohammedanism, was born at Mecca (20 August?) A.D. 570. Arabia was then torn by warring factions. The tribe of Fihr, or Quraish, to which Mohammed belonged, had established itself in the south of Hijâs (Hedjaz), near Mecca, which was, even then, the principal religious and commercial centre of Arabia. The power of the tribe was continually increasing; they had become the masters and the acknowledged guardians of the sacred Kaaba, within the town of Mecca — then visited in annual pilgrimage by the heathen Arabs with their offerings and tributes — and had thereby gained such preeminence that it was comparatively easy for Mohammed to inaugurate his religious reform and his political campaign, which ended with the conquest of all Arabia and the fusion of the numerous Arab tribes into one nation, with one religion, one code, and one sanctuary. (See *Christianity in Arabia.*)

Mohammed's father was Abdallah, of the family of Hashim, who died soon after his son's birth. At the age of six the boy lost his mother and was thereafter taken care of by his uncle Abu-Talib. He spent his early life as a shepherd and an attendant of caravans, and at the age of twenty-five married a rich widow, Khadeejah, fifteen years his senior. She bore him six children, all of whom died very young except Fatima, his beloved daughter.

On his commercial journeys to Syria and Palestine he became acquainted with Jews and Christians, and acquired an imperfect knowledge of their religion and traditions. He was a man of retiring disposition, addicted to prayer and fasting, and was subject to epileptic fits. In his fortieth year (A.D. 610), he claimed to have received a call from the Angel Gabriel, and thus began his active career as the prophet of Allah and the apostle of Arabia. His first converts were about forty in all, including his wife, his daughter, his father-in-law Abu Bakr, his adopted son Ali Omar, and his slave Zayd. By his preaching and his attack on heathenism, Mohammed provoked persecution which drove him from Mecca to Medina in 622, the year of the Hejira (Flight) and the beginning of the Mohammedan Era. At Medina he was recognized as the prophet of God, and his followers increased. He took the field against his enemies, conquered several Arabian, Jewish, and Christian tribes, entered Mecca in triumph in 630, demolished the idols of the Caaba, became master of Arabia, and finally united all the tribes under one emblem and one religion. In 632 he made his last pilgrimage to Mecca at the head of forty thousand followers, and soon after his return died of a violent fever in the sixty-third year of his age, the eleventh of the Hejira, and the year 633 of the Christian era.

The sources of Mohammed's biography are numerous, but on the whole untrustworthy, being crowded with fictitious details, legends, and stories. None of his biographies were compiled during his lifetime, and the earliest was written a century and a half after his death. The Koran is perhaps the only reliable source for the leading events in his career. His earliest and chief biographers are Ibn Ishaq (A.H. 151=A.D. 768), Wakidi (207=822), Ibn Hisham (213=828), Ibn Sa'd (230=845), Tirmidhi (279=892), Tabari (310=929), the "Lives of the Companions of Mohammed", the numerous Koranic commentators [especially Tabari, quoted above, Zamakhshari (538=1144), and Baidawi (691=1292)], the "Musnad", or collection of traditions of Ahmad ibn Hanbal (241=855), the collections of Bokhari (256=870), the "Isabah", or "Dictionary of Persons who knew

Mohammed", by Ibn Hajar, etc. All these collections and biographies are based on the so-called Hadiths, or "traditions", the historical value of which is more than doubtful.

These traditions, in fact, represent a gradual, and more or less artificial, legendary development, rather than supplementary historical information. According to them, Mohammed was simple in his habits, but most careful of his personal appearance. He loved perfumes and hated strong drink. Of a highly nervous temperament, he shrank from bodily pain. Though gifted with great powers of imagination, he was taciturn. He was affectionate and magnanimous, pious and austere in the practice of his religion, brave, zealous, and above reproach in his personal and family conduct. Palgrave, however, wisely remarks that "the ideals of Arab virtue were first conceived and then attributed to him". Nevertheless, with every allowance for exaggeration, Mohammed is shown by his life and deeds to have been a man of dauntless courage, great generalship, strong patriotism, merciful by nature, and quick to forgive. And yet he was ruthless in his dealings with the Jews, when once he had ceased to hope for their submission. He approved of assassination, when it furthered his cause; however barbarous or treacherous the means, the end justified it in his eyes; and in more than one case he not only approved, but also instigated the crime.

Concerning his moral character and sincerity contradictory opinions have been expressed by scholars in the last three centuries. Many of these opinions are biased either by an extreme hatred of Islam and its founder or by an exaggerated admiration, coupled with a hatred of Christianity. Luther looked upon him as "a devil and first-born child of Satan". Maracci held that Mohammed and Mohammedanism were not very dissimilar to Luther and Protestantism. Spanheim and D'Herbelot characterize him as a "wicked impostor", and a "dastardly liar", while Prideaux stamps him as a wilful deceiver. Such indiscriminate abuse is unsupported by facts. Modern scholars, such as Sprenger, Nöldeke, Weil, Muir, Koelle, Grimme, Margoliouth, give us a more correct and unbiased estimate of Mohammed's life and character, and substantially agree as to his motives, prophetic call, personal qualifications, and sincerity. The various estimates of several recent critics have been ably collected and summarized by Zwemer, in his "Islam, a Challenge to Faith" (New York, 1907). According to Sir William Muir, Marcus Dods, and some others, Mohammed was at first sincere, but later, carried away by success, he practised deception wherever it would gain his end. Koelle "finds the key to the first period of Mohammed's life in Khadija, his first wife", after

15

whose death he became a prey to his evil passions. Sprenger attributes the alleged revelations to epileptic fits, or to "a paroxysm of cataleptic insanity". Zwemer himself goes on to criticize the life of Mohammed by the standards, first, of the Old and New Testaments, both of which Mohammed acknowledged as Divine revelation; second, by the pagan morality of his Arabian compatriots; lastly, by the new law of which he pretended to be the "divinely appointed medium and custodian". According to this author, the prophet was false even to the ethical traditions of the idolatrous brigands among whom he lived, and grossly violated the easy sexual morality of his own system. After this, it is hardly necessary to say that, in Zwemer's opinion, Mohammed fell very far short of the most elementary requirements of Scriptural morality. Quoting Johnstone, Zwemer concludes by remarking that the judgment of these modern scholars, however harsh, rests on evidence which "comes all from the lips and the pens of his own devoted adherents.... And the followers of the prophet can scarcely complain if, even on such evidence, the verdict of history goes against him".

The System

A. Geographical Extent, Divisions, and Distribution of Mohammedans

After Mohammed's death Mohammedanism aspired to become a world power and a universal religion. The weakness of the Byzantine Empire, the unfortunate rivalry between the Greek and Latin Churches, the schisms of Nestorius and Eutyches, the failing power of the Sassanian dynasty of Persia, the lax moral code of the new religion, the power of the sword and of fanaticism, the hope of plunder and the love of conquest — all these factors combined with the genius of the caliphs, the successors of Mohammed, to effect the conquest, in considerably less than a century, of Palestine, Syria, Mesopotamia, Egypt, North Africa, and the South of Spain. The Moslems even crossed the Pyrenees, threatening to stable their horses in St. Peter's at Rome, but were at last defeated by Charles Martel at Tours, in 732, just one hundred years from the death of Mohammed. This defeat arrested their western conquests and saved Europe. In the eighth and ninth centuries they conquered Persia, Afghanistan, and a large part of India, and in the twelfth century they had already become the absolute masters of all Western Asia, Spain and North Africa, Sicily, etc. They were finally conquered by the Mongols and Turks, in the thirteenth century, but the new conquerors adopted Mohammed's religion and, in the fifteenth century, overthrew the tottering Byzantine Empire (1453). From that stronghold (Constantinople) they even threatened the German Empire, but were successfully defeated at the gates of Vienna, and driven back across the Danube, in 1683.

Mohammedanism now comprises various theological schools and political factions. The Orthodox (Sunni) uphold the legitimacy of the succession of the first three caliphs, Abu Bakr, Omar, and Uthman, while the Schismatics (Shiah) champion the Divine right of Ali as against the successions of these caliphs whom they call "usurpers", and whose names, tombs, and memorials they insult and detest. The Shiah number at present about twelve million adherents, or about one-twentieth of the whole Mohammedan world, and are scattered over Persia and India. The Sunni are subdivided into four principal theological schools, or sects, viz., the Hanifites, found mostly in Turkey, Central Asia, and Northern India; the Shafiites in Southern India and Egypt; the Malikites, in Morocco, Barbary, and parts of Arabia; and the Hanbalites in Central and Eastern Arabia and in some parts of Africa. The Shiah are also subdivided into various, but less important, sects. Of the proverbial seventy-three sects of

Islam, thirty-two are assigned to the Shiah. The principal differences between the two are: (1) as to the legitimate successors of Mohammed; (2) the Shiah observe the ceremonies of the month of fasting, Muharram, in commemoration of Ali, Hasan, Husain, and Bibi Fatimah, whilst the Sunnites only regard the tenth day of that month as sacred, and as being the day on which God created Adam and Eve; (3) the Shiah permit temporary marriages, contracted for a certain sum of money, whilst the Sunnites maintain that Mohammed forbade them; (4) the Shi'ites include the Fire-Worshippers among the "People of the Book", whilst the Sunnites acknowledge only Jews, Christians, and Moslems as such; (5) several minor differences in the ceremonies of prayer and ablution; (6) the Shiah admit a principle of religious compromise in order to escape persecution and death, whilst the Sunni regard this as apostasy.

There are also minor sects, the principal of which are the Aliites, or Fatimites, the Asharians, Azaragites, Babakites, Babis, Idrisites, Ismailians and Assassins, Jabrians, Kaissanites, Karmathians, Kharijites, followers of the Mahdi, Mu'tazilites, Qadrians, Safrians, Sifatians, Sufis, Wahabis, and Zaidites. The distinctive features of these various sects are political as well as religious; only three or four of them now possess any influence.

In spite of these divisions, however, the principal

articles of faith and morality, and the ritual, are substantially uniform.

According to the latest and most reliable accounts (1907), the number of Mohammedans in the world is about 233 millions, although some estimate the number as high as 300 millions, others, again, as low as 175 millions. Nearly 60 millions are in Africa, 170 millions in Asia, and about 5 millions in Europe. Their total number amounts to about one-fourth of the population of Asia, and one-seventh that of the whole world. Their geographical distribution is as follows:

Asia

India, 62 millions; other British possessions (such as Aden, Bahrein, Ceylon, and Cyprus), about one million and a half; Russia (Asiatic and European), the Caucasus, Russian Turkestan, and the Amur region, about 13 millions; Philippine Islands, 350,000; Dutch East Indies (including Java, Sumatra, Borneo, Celebes, etc.) about 30 millions; French possessions in Asia (Pondicherry, Annam, Cambodia, Cochin-China, Tongking, Laos), about one million and a half; Bokhara, 1,200,000; Khiva, 800,000; Persia, 8,800,000; Afghanistan, 4,000,000; China and Chinese Turkestan, 30,000,000; Japan and Formosa, 30,000; Korea, 10,000; Siam, 1,000,000; Asia Minor, 7,179,000; Armenia and

Kurdistan, 1,795,000; Mesopotamia, 1,200,000; Syria, 1,100,000; Arabia, 4,500,000. Total, 170,000,000.

Africa

Egypt, 9,000,000; Tripoli, 1,250,000; Tunis, 1,700,000; Algeria, 4,000,000; Morocco, 5,600,000; Eritrea, 150,000; Anglo-Egyptian Sudan, 1,000,000; Senegambia-Niger, 18,000,000; Abyssinia, 350,000; Kamerun, 2,000,000; Nigeria, 6,000,000; Dahomey, 350,000; Ivory Coast, 800,000; Liberia, 600,000; Sierra Leone, 333,000; French Guinea, 1,500,000; French, British, and Italian Somaliland, British East African Protectorate, Uganda, Togoland, Gambia and Senegal, about 2,000,000; Zanzibar, German East Africa, Portuguese East Africa, Rhodesia, Congo Free State, and French Congo, about 4,000,000; South Africa and adjacent islands, about 235,000. — Approximate total, 60,000,000.

Europe

Turkey in Europe, 2,100,000; Greece, Servia, Rumania, and Bulgaria, about 1,369,000. Total, about 3,500,000.

America and Australia

About 70,000.

About 7,000,000 (i.e., four-fifths) of the Persian Mohammedans and about 5,000,000 of the Indian Mohammedans are Shiahs; the rest of the Mohammedan world — about 221,000,000 — are almost all Sunnites.

B. Tenets

The principal tenets of Mohammedanism are laid down in the Koran. As aids in interpreting the religious system of the Koran we have: *first*, the so-called "Traditions", which are supposed to contain supplementary teachings and doctrine of Mohammed, a very considerable part of which, however, is decidedly spurious; *second*, the consensus of the doctors of Islam represented by the most celebrated imâms, the founders of the various Islamic sects, the Koranic commentators and the masters of Mohammedan jurisprudence; *third*, the analogy, or deduction from recognized principles admitted in the Koran and in the Traditions. Mohammed's religion, known among its adherents as Islam, contains practically nothing original; it is a confused combination of native Arabian heathenism, Judaism, Christianity, Sabiism (Mandoeanism), Hanifism, and Zoroastrianism.

The system may be divided into two parts: dogma, or theory; and morals, or practice. The whole fabric is built on five fundamental points, one belonging to faith, or theory, and the other four to morals, or practice. All Mohammedan dogma is supposed to be expressed in the one formula: "There is no God but the true God; and Mohammed is His prophet." But this one confession implies for Mohammedans six distinct articles: (a) belief in the unity of God; (b) in His angels; (c) in His Scripture; (d) in His prophets; (e) in the Resurrection and Day of Judgment; and (f) in God's absolute and irrevocable decree and predetermination both of good and of evil. The four points relating to morals, or practice, are: (a) prayer, ablutions, and purifications; (b) alms: (c) fasting; and (d) pilgrimage to Mecca.

(1) Dogma

The doctrines of Islam concerning God — His unity and Divine attributes — are essentially those of the Bible; but to the doctrines of the Trinity and of the Divine Sonship of Christ Mohammed had the strongest antipathy. As Nöldeke remarks, Mohammed's acquaintance with those two dogmas was superficial; even the clauses of the Creed that referred to them were not properly known to him, and thus he felt that it was quite impossible to bring them into harmony with the simple Semitic Monotheism; probably, too, it was this consideration alone that hindered him from embracing Christianity (*Sketches from Eastern History*, 62).

The number of prophets sent by God is said to have been about 124,000, and of apostles, 315. Of the former, 22 are mentioned by name in the Koran — such as Adam, Noe, Abraham, Moses, Jesus.

According to the Sunni, the Prophets and Apostles were sinless and superior to the angels, and they had the power of performing miracles. Mohammedan angelology and demonology are almost wholly based on later Jewish and early Christian traditions. The angels are believed to be free from all sin; they neither eat nor drink; there is no distinction of sex among them. They are, as a rule, invisible, save to animals, although, at times, they appear in human form. The principal angels are: Gabriel, the guardian and communicator of God's revelation to man; Michael, the guardian of men; Azrail, the angel of death, whose duty is to receive men's souls when they die; and Israfil, the angel of the Resurrection. In addition to these there are the Seraphim, who surround the throne of God, constantly chanting His praises; the Secretaries, who record the actions of men; the Observers, who spy on every word and deed of mankind; the Travellers, whose duty it is to traverse the whole earth in order to know whether, and when, men utter the name of God; the Angels of the Seven Planets; the Angels who have charge of hell; and a countless multitude of heavenly beings who fill all space. The chief devil is Iblîs, who, like his numerous companions, was once the nearest to God, but was cast out for refusing to pay homage to Adam at the command of God. These devils are harmful both to the souls and to the bodies of men, although their evil influence is constantly checked by Divine interference. Besides angels and devils, there are also jinns, or genii, creatures of fire, able to eat, drink, propagate, and die; some good, others bad, but all capable of future salvation and damnation.

God rewards good and punishes evil deeds. He is merciful and is easily propitiated by repentance. The punishment of the impenitent wicked will be fearful, and the reward of the faithful great. All men will have to rise from the dead and submit to the universal judgment. The Day of Resurrection and of Judgment will be preceded and accompanied by seventeen fearful, or greater, signs in heaven and on earth, and eight lesser ones, some of which are identical with those mentioned in the New Testament. The Resurrection will be general and will extend to all creatures — angels, jinns, men, and brutes. The torments of hell and the pleasures of Paradise, but especially the latter, are proverbially crass and sensual. Hell is divided into seven regions: Jahannam, reserved for faithless Mohammedans; Laza, for the Jews; Al-

Hutama, for the Christians; Al-Sair, for the Sabians; Al-Saqar, for the Magians; Al-Jahîm, for idolaters; Al-Hâwiyat, for hypocrites. As to the torments of hell, it is believed that the damned will dwell amid pestilential winds and in scalding water, and in the shadow of a black smoke. Draughts of boiling water will be forced down their throats. They will be dragged by the scalp, flung into the fire, wrapped in garments of flame, and beaten with iron maces. When their skins are well burned, other skins will be given them for their greater torture. While the damnation of all infidels will be hopeless and eternal, the Moslems, who, though holding the true religion, have been guilty of heinous sins, will be delivered from hell after expiating their crimes.

The joys and glories of Paradise are as fantastic and sensual as the lascivious Arabian mind could possibly imagine. "As plenty of water is one of the greatest additions to the delights of the Bedouin Arab, the Koran often speaks of the rivers of Paradise as a principal ornament thereof; some of these streams flow with water, some with wine and others with honey, besides many other lesser springs and fountains, whose pebbles are rubies and emeralds, while their earth consists of camphor, their beds of musk, and their sides of saffron. But all these glories will be eclipsed by the resplendent and ravishing girls, or *houris*, of Paradise, the enjoyment of whose company will be the principal felicity of the faithful. These maidens are created not of clay, as in the case of mortal women, but of pure musk, and free from all natural impurities, defects, and inconveniences. They will be beautiful and modest and secluded from public view in pavilions of hollow pearls. The pleasures of Paradise will be so overwhelming that God will give to everyone the potentialities of a hundred individuals. To each individuals a large mansion will be assigned, and the very meanest will have at his disposal at least 80,000 servants and seventy-two wives of the girls of Paradise. While eating they will be waited on by 300 attendants, the food being served in dishes of gold, whereof 300 shall be set before him at once, containing each a different kind of food, and an inexhaustible supply of wine and liquors. The magnificence of the garments and gems is conformable to the delicacy of their diet. For they will be clothed in the richest silks and brocades, and adorned with bracelets of gold and silver, and crowns set with pearls, and will make use of silken carpets, couches, pillows, etc., and in order that they may enjoy all these pleasures, God will grant them perpetual youth, beauty, and vigour. Music and singing will also be ravishing and everlasting" (Wollaston, "Muhammed, His Life and Doctrines").

The Mohammedan doctrine of predestination is

equivalent to fatalism. They believe in God's absolute decree and predetermination both of good and of evil; viz., whatever has been or shall be in the world, whether good or bad, proceeds entirely from the Divine will, and is irrevocably fixed and recorded from all eternity. The possession and the exercise of our own free will is, accordingly, futile and useless. The absurdity of this doctrine was felt by later Mohammedan theologians, who sought in vain by various subtle distinctions to minimize it.

(2) Practice

The five pillars of the practical and of the ritualistic side of Islam are the recital of the Creed and prayers, fasting, almsgiving, and the pilgrimage to Mecca. The formula of the Creed has been given above, and its recital is necessary for salvation. The daily prayers are five in number: before sunrise, at midday, at four in the afternoon, at sunset, and shortly before midnight. The forms of prayer and the postures are prescribed in a very limited Koranic liturgy. All prayers must be made looking towards Mecca, and must be preceded by washing, neglect of which renders the prayers of no effect. Public prayer is made on Friday in the mosque, and is led by an imâm. Only men attend the public prayers, as women seldom pray even at home. Prayers for the dead are meritorious and commended. Fasting is commended at all seasons, but prescribed only in the month of Ramadan. It begins at sunrise and ends at sunset, and is very rigorous, especially when the fasting season falls in summer. At the end of Ramadan comes the great feast-day, generally called Bairam, or Fitr, i.e., "Breaking of the Fast". The other great festival is that of Azha, borrowed with modifications from the Jewish Day of Atonement. Almsgiving is highly commended: on the feast-day after Ramadan it is obligatory, and is to be directed to the "faithful" (Mohammedans) only. Pilgrimage to Mecca once in a lifetime is a duty incumbent on every free Moslem of sufficient means and bodily strength; the merit of it cannot be obtained by deputy, and the ceremonies are strictly similar to those performed by the Prophet himself. Pilgrimages to the tombs of saints are very common nowadays, especially in Persia and India, although they were absolutely forbidden by Mohammed.

It is hardly necessary here to emphasize the fact that the ethics of Islam are far inferior to those of Judaism and even more inferior to those of the New Testament. Furthermore, we cannot agree with Nöldeke when he maintains that, although in many respects the ethics of Islam are not to be compared even with such Christianity as prevailed, and still prevails, in the East, nevertheless, in other points, the new faith — simple, robust, in the vigour of its youth — far surpassed the religion of the Syrian and Egyptian Christians, which was in a stagnating condition, and steadily sinking lower and lower into the depths of barbarism (op. cit., Wollaston, 71, 72). The history and the development, as well as the past and present religious, social, and ethical condition of all the Christian nations and countries, no matter of what sect or school they may be, as compared with these of the various Mohammedan countries, in all ages, is a sufficient refutation of Nöldeke's assertion. That in the ethics of Islam there is a great deal to admire and to approve, is beyond dispute; but of originality or superiority, there is none. What is really good in Mohammedan ethics is either commonplace or borrowed from some other religions, whereas what is characteristic is nearly always imperfect or wicked.

The principal sins forbidden by Mohammed are idolatry and apostasy, adultery, false witness against a brother Moslem, games of chance, the drinking of wine or other intoxicants, usury, and divination by arrows. Brotherly love is confined in Islam to Mohammedans. Any form of idolatry or apostasy is severely punished in Islam, but the violation of any of the other ordinances is generally allowed to go unpunished, unless it seriously conflicts with the social welfare or the political order of the State. Among other prohibitions mention must be made of the eating of blood, of swine's flesh, of whatever dies of itself, or is slain in honour of any idol, or is strangled, or killed by a blow, or a fall, or by another beast. In case of dire necessity, however, these restrictions may be dispensed with. Infanticide, extensively practiced by the pre-Islamic Arabs, is strictly forbidden by Mohammed, as is also the sacrificing of children to idols in fulfilment of vows, etc. The crime of infanticide commonly took the form of burying newborn females, lest the parents should be reduced to poverty by providing for them, or else that they might avoid the sorrow and disgrace which would follow, if their daughters should be made captives or become scandalous by their behaviour.

Religion and the State are not separated in Islam. Hence Mohammedan jurisprudence, civil and criminal, is mainly based on the Koran and on the "Traditions". Thousands of judicial decisions are attributed to Mohammed and incorporated in the various collections of Hadith. Mohammed commanded reverence and obedience to parents, and kindness to wives and slaves. Slander and backbiting are strongly denounced, although false evidence is allowed to hide a Moslem's crime and to save his reputation or life. As regards marriage, polygamy, and divorce, the Koran explicitly (sura iv, v. 3) allows four lawful wives at a time, whom the husband may divorce whenever he pleases. Slave-mistresses and concubines are permitted in any number. At present, however, owing to economic reasons, concubinage is not as commonly practiced as Western popular opinion seems to hold. Seclusion of wives is commanded, and in case of unfaithfulness, the wife's evidence, either in her own defense or against her husband, is not admitted, while that of the husband invariably is. In this, as in other judicial cases, the evidence of two women, if admitted, is sometimes allowed to be worth that of one man. The man is allowed to repudiate his wife on the slightest pretext, but the woman is not permitted even to separate herself from her husband unless it be for ill-usage, want of proper maintenance, or neglect of conjugal duty; and even then she generally loses her dowry, when she does not if divorced by her husband, unless she has been guilty of immodesty or notorious disobedience. Both husband and wife are explicitly forbidden by Mohammed to seek divorce on any slight occasion or the prompting of a whim, but this warning was not heeded either by Mohammed himself or by his followers. A divorced wife, in order to ascertain the paternity of a possible or probable offspring, must wait three months before she marries again. A widow, on the other hand, must wait four months and ten days. Immorality in general is severely condemned and punished by the Koran, but the moral laxity and depraved sensualism of the Mohammedans at large have practically nullified Koranic ethics.

Slavery is not only tolerated in the Koran, but is looked upon as a practical necessity, while the manumission of slaves is regarded as a meritorious deed. It must be observed, however, that among Mohammedans, the children of slaves and of concubines are generally considered equally legitimate with those of legal wives, none being accounted bastards except such as are born of public prostitutes, and whose fathers are unknown. The accusation often brought against the Koran that it teaches that women have no souls is without foundation. The Koranic law concerning inheritance insists that women and orphans be treated with justice and kindness. Generally speaking, however, males are entitled to twice as much as females. Contracts are to be conscientiously drawn up in the presence of witnesses. Murder, manslaughter, and suicide are explicitly forbidden, although blood revenge is allowed. In case of personal injury, the law of retaliation is approved.

In conclusion, reference must be made here to the sacred months, and to the weekly holy day. The Arabs had a year of twelve lunar months, and this, as often as seemed necessary, they brought roughly into accordance with the solar year by the intercalation of a thirteenth month. The Mohammedan year, however, has a mean duration of 354 days, and is ten or eleven days shorter than the solar year, and Mohammedan festivals, accordingly, move in succession through all the seasons. The Mohammedan Era begins with the Hegira, which is assumed to have taken place on the 16th day of July, A.D. 622. To find what year of the Christian Era (A.D.) is represented by a given year of the Mohammedan Era (A.H.), the rule is: Subtract from the Mohammedan date the product of three times the last completed number of centuries, and add 621 to the remainder. (This rule, however, gives an exact result only for the first day of a Mohammedan century. Thus, e.g., the first day of the fourteenth century came in the course of the year of Our Lord 1883.) The first, seventh, eleventh and twelfth months of the Mohammedan year are sacred; during these months it is not lawful to wage war. The twelfth month is consecrated to the annual pilgrimage to Mecca, and, in order to protect pilgrims, the preceding (eleventh) month and the following (first of the new year) are also inviolable. The seventh month is reserved for the fast which Mohammed substituted for a month (the ninth) devoted by the Arabs in pre-Islamic times to excessive eating and drinking. Mohammed selected Friday as the sacred day of the week, and several fanciful reasons are adduced by the Prophet himself and by his followers for the selection; the most probable motive was the desire to have a holy day different from that of the Jews and that of the Christians. It is certain, however, that Friday was a day of solemn gatherings and public festivities among the pre-Islamic Arabs. Abstinence from work is not enjoined on Friday, but it is commanded that public prayers and worship must be performed on that day. Another custom dating from antiquity and still universally observed by all Mohammedans, although not explicitly enjoined in the Koran, is circumcision. It is looked upon as a semi-religious practice, and its performance is preceded and accompanied by great festivities.

In matters political Islam is a system of despotism at home and aggression abroad. The Prophet commanded absolute submission to the imâm. In no case was the sword to be raised against him. The rights of non-Moslem subjects are of the vaguest and most limited kind, and a religious war is a sacred duty whenever there is a chance of success against the "Infidel". Medieval and modern Mohammedan, especially Turkish, persecutions of both Jews and Christians are perhaps the best illustration of this fanatical religious and political spirit.

Moslems

SPRENGER, *Das Leben und die Lehre des Mohammed* (Berlin, 1865); WEIL, *Das Leben Mohammed* (Stuttgart, 1864); MUIR, *Life of Mohammed* (London, 1858, 1897); IDEM, *Mohammed and Islam* (London, 1887), SYED AMEER ALI, *A Critical Examination of the Life and Teachings of Mohammed* (London, 1873); IDEM, *The Spirit of Islam; or, The Life and Teaching of Mohammed* (Calcutta, 1902); KOELLE, *Mohammed and Mohammedanism Critically Considered* (London, 1888); NÖLDEKE, *Das Leben Muhammeds* (Hanover, 1863); IDEM, *Islam in Sketches from Eastern History* (London, 1892), 61-106; WELLHAUSEN, *Muhammed in Medina* (Berlin, 1882); KREHL, *Mohammed* (Leipzig, 1884); GRIMME, *Mohammed* (2 vols., Münster, 1892-94); MARGOLIOUTH, *Mohammed and the Rise of Islam* (London, 1905); ZWEMER, *Islam a Challenge to Faith* (New York, 1907); CAETANI, *Annali dell' Islam* (Milan, 1905-); MARACCI, *Prodromi ad refutationem Alcorani* (4 parts, Padua, 1698); ARNOLD, *Islam, its History, Character, and Relation to Christianity* (London, 1874); KREMER, *Geschichte der herrschenden Ideen des Islams* (Leipzig, 1868); IDEM, *Culturgeschichte des Orients unter den Chalifen* (2 vols., Vienna, 1875-77); HUGHES, *Dictionary of Islam* (London, 1895); IDEM, *Notes on Mohammedanism* (3rd ed., London, 1894); MUIR, *The Coran, its Composition and Teaching* (London, 1878); PERRON, *L'Islamisme, son institution, son état actuel et son avenir* (Paris, 1877); GARCIN DE TASSY, *L'Islamisme d'aprés le Coran, l'enseignement doctrinal et la pratique* (2nd ed., Paris, 1874); MÜLLER, *Der Islam im Morgen- und Abendland* (2 vols., Berlin, 1885-87); GOLDZIHER, *Muhammedanische Studien* (2 vols., Halle, 1889-98); IDEM in *Die Orientalischen Religionen* (Leipzig, 1905), 87-135; LHEREUX, *Etude sur l'Islamisme* (Geneva, 1904); *Encyclopedia of Islam* (Leyden and London, 1908-); SMITH, *Mohammed and Mohammedanism* (London, 1876); KREHL, *Beiträge zur Muhammedanischen Dogmatik* (Leipzig, 1885); TOOL, *Studies in Mohammedanism, Historical and Doctrinal* (London, 1892); SELL, *The Faith of Islam* (London, 1886); WOLLASTON, *Muhammed, His Life and Doctrines* (London,

1904); IDEM, *The Sword of Islam* (New York, 1905); JOHNSTONE, *Muhammed and His Power* (New York, 1901); *Literary Remains of the Late Emanuel Deutsch* (London, 1874), 59-135; PIZZI, *L'Islamismo* (Milan, 1905); ARNOLD, *The Preaching of Islam, A History of the Propagation of the Muslim Faith* (London, 1896); MACDONALD, *Development of Muslim Theology, Jurisprudence, and Constitutional Theory* (New York, 1903); IDEM, *The Religious Attitude and Life in Islam* (Chicago, 1908); ZWEMER, *The Mohammedan World To-day* (New York, 1906); CARRA DE VAUX, *La doctrine de l'Islam* (Paris, 1909); LAMMENS, *A travers l'Islam in Etudes* (Paris, 20 Oct., 1910); MARES, *Les Musulmans dans l'Inde*, ibid. (Jan. 5 and 20).

GABRIEL OUSSANI

Islam

Islam, an Arabic word which, since Mohammed's time, has acquired a religious and technical significance denoting the religion of Mohammed and of the Koran, just as Christianity denotes that of Jesus and of the Gospels, or Judaism that of Moses, the Prophets, and of the Old Testament.

Grammatically, the word *Islam* is the infinitive of the so-called fourth verbal form of the regular intransitive stem *salima*, "to be safe", "to be secure", etc. In its second verbal form (*sallama*) it means "to make some one safe" and "to free", "to make secure", etc. In its third form (*salama*), it signifies "to make peace", or "to become at peace", i.e., "to be reconciled". In its fourth form (*aslama*), the infinitive of which is *islam*, it acquires the sense of "to resign", "to submit oneself" or "to surrender". Hence Islam, in its ethico-religious significance, means the "entire surrender of the will to God", and its professors are called Muslimun (sing. Muslim), which is the participial form, that is "those who have surrendered themselves", or "believers", as opposed to the "rejectors" of the Divine message, who are called Kafirs, Mushriks (that is those who associate various gods with the Deity), or pagans. Historically, of course, to become a Muslim was to become a follower of Mohammed and of his religion; and it is very doubtful whether the earliest Muslims or followers of Mohammed, had any clear notion of the ethico-religious significance of the term, although its later theological development is entirely consistent and logical. According to the Shafiites (one of the four great Mohammedan schools of theology), Islam, as a priniciple of the law of God, is "the manifesting of humility or submission, and outward conforming with the law of God, and the taking upon oneself to do or to say as the Prophet has done or said"; and if this outward manifestation of religion is coupled with "a firm and internal belief of the heart", i.e., faith, then it is called Iman. Hence the Mohammedan theological axiom "Islam is with the tongue, and Iman is with the heart." According to the Hanafites (another of the four above-mentioned schools), however, no distinction is to be made between the two terms, as Iman, according to them, is essentially included in Islam.

Islam is sometimes divided under two heads of "Faith", or "Iman", and "Practical Religion", or "Din". Faith (Iman) includes a belief in one God, omnipotent, omniscient, all-merciful, the author of all good, and in Mohammed as His prophet, expressed in the formula: "There is no God but God, and Mohammed is the Prophet of God." It includes also, belief in the authority and sufficiency of the Koran, in angels, genii, and the devil, in the immortality of the soul, the resurrection, the day of judgment, and in God's absolute decree for good and evil. Practical religion (Din), on the other hand, consists of five observances, viz.: recital of the formula of belief, prayer with ablution, fasting, almsgiving, and the pilgrimage to Mecca. For further details see KORAN and MOHAMMEDANISM.

GABRIEL OUSSANI

Koran

The sacred book of the Muslims, by whom it is regarded as the revelation of God. Supplemented by the so-called *Hadith*, or traditions, it is the foundation of Islam and the final authority in dogma and belief, in jurisprudence, worship, ethics, and in social, family, and individual conduct. The name *Koran*, or better *Qur'ân*, from the Arabic stem Qara'a, "to read", "to recite", means the "Reading", the "Recitation", i.e., the "Book", *par excellence*. It is also called — to select a few of many titles — "Alkitâb" (The Book), "Furqan" ("liberation", "deliverance", of the revelation), "Kitab-ul-lâh" (Book of God), "Al-tanzîl" (The Revelation). It consists of one hundred and fourteen suras or chapters, some being almost as long as the Book of Genesis, others consisting of but two or three sentences. It is smaller than the New Testament, and in its present form has no chronological order or logical sequence.

Contents and Analysis

The Koran contains dogma, legends, history, fiction, religion and superstition, social and family laws, prayers, threats, liturgy, fanciful descriptions of heaven, hell, the judgment day, resurrection, etc. — a combination of fact and fancy often devoid of force and originality. The most creditable portions are those in which Jewish and Christian influences are clearly discernible. The following analysis is based on Sir William Muir's chronological arrangement (op. cit. *infra*).

First Period

Suras 103, 91, 106, 101, 95, 102, 104, 82, 92, 105, rhapsodies, which may have been composed before Mohammed conceived the idea of a Divine mission, or of a revelation direct from Heaven.

Second Period (the opening of Mohammed's ministry)

Sura 96, the command to "recite in the name of the Lord"; sura 113, on the unity and eternity of the Deity; sura 74, the command to preach, the denunciation of one of the chiefs of Mecca who scoffed at the resurrection, unbelievers threatened with hell; sura 111,

Abu Lahab (the Prophet's uncle) and his wife are cursed.

Third Period (from the beginning of Mohammed's public ministry to the Abyssinian emigration)

Suras 87, 97, 88, 80, 81, 84, 86, 90, 85, 83, 78, 77, 76, 75, 70, 109, 107, 55, 56, descriptions of the resurrection, paradise, and hell, with references to the growing opposition of the Koreish tribe.

Fourth Period (from the sixth to the tenth year of Mohammed's ministry)

Suras 67, 53, 32, 39, 73, 79, 54, 34, 31, 69, 68, 41, 71, 52, 50, 45, 44, 37, 30, 26, 15, 51, narratives from the Jewish Scriptures and from rabbinical and Arab legends; the temporary compromise with idolatry is connected with sura 53.

Fifth Period (from the tenth year of Mohammed's ministry to the Flight from Mecca)

Suras 46, 72, 35, 36, 19, 18, 27, 42, 40, 38, 25, 20, 43, 12, 11, 10, 14, 6, 64, 28, 22, 21, 17, 16, 13, 29, 7, 113, 114. The suras of this period contain some narratives from the Gospel, enjoin the rites of pilgrimage, refute the cavillings of the Koreish, and contain vivid descriptions of the resurrection, judgment, heaven, and hell, with proofs of God's unity, power, and providence. Gradually the suras become longer, some of them filling many pages. In the later suras of the fifth period Medina passages are often interpolated.

Last Period (suras revealed at Medina)

This period includes the following suras:

Sura 98: on good and bad Jews and Christians. Sura 2, the longest in the Koran, is called the "Sura of the Cow" from the red heifer described in verse 67 as having been sacrificed by the Israelites at the direction of Moses. It is a collection of passages on various subjects, delivered during the first two or three years after the Flight. The greater portion relates to the Jews, who are sometimes exhorted and sometimes reprobated. Biblical and rabbinical stories abound. This sura contains the order to change the Qibla (or direction at prayer) a denunciation of the disaffected citizens of Medina, injunctions to fight, permission to bear arms in the sacred months and much matter of a legislative character promulgated on first reaching Medina, with passages of a later date interpolated. Sura 3 belongs partly to the time immediately after the

Battle of Behr. The Jews are referred to in terms of hostility. The interview with Christian deputation from Najrân (verses 57-63) is of a later date. Passages pertaining to the farewell pilgrimage are introduced with other (probably) earlier texts on the rites of pilgrimage. Sura 8 contains instructions on the division of spoil at Bedr. Some parts are in the old Meccan style and the Koreish are frequently referred to. In sura 47 war and slaughter are enjoined, and idolaters of Mecca threatened. In sura 62 the Jews are denounced for their ignorance; the Friday service is to take precedence of secular engagements. In sura 5 the Jews are reviled; the doctrines of the Christians are controverted; it contains also civil ordinances and miscellaneous instructions. Sura 59, on the siege and expulsion of the Banu Nadhir. Sura 4 is entitled "women", from the large portion devoted to the treatment of wives and relation of sexes. There are also ordinances on the law of inheritance and general precepts, social and political. Idolatrous Meccans are to be shunned, and there are animadversions against the Jews. Sura 58: on divorce and other social questions. The "disaffected" are blamed for taking the part of the Jews. Sura 65: on divorce and kindred subjects, with some religious observations. Sura 63: menaces against 'Abdallah ibn Obey for his treasonable language on the expedition against the Banu Mustalick. Sura 24: vindication of

'Ayisha, with the law of evidence for conjugal unfaithfulness, and miscellaneous precepts. Sura 33, composed of portions covering the year A. H. 5. The marriage of the Prophet with Zeinab, wife of his adopted son, is sanctioned. There are various passages on the conjugal relations of Mohammed, the siege of Medina, and the fall of the Banu Qoreitza. Sura 57: injunctions to fight and contribute towards the expenses of war. The disaffected are warned. Christians are mentioned in kindly terms. Sura 61: on war; speedy victory is promised. — The remaining suras belong exclusively to the last five years of the Prophet's life. Sura 48 refers to the truce of Hodeibia, and the prospect of victory and spoil to be obtained elsewhere. Sura 60: on the treatment of the women who, after the truce, came over from Mecca; idolaters of Mecca to be shunned. Sura 66: on the affair of Mohammed and the Coptic maid. Sura 49: blaming the profession of the Bedouin Arabs as insincere, chiding the deputation which called out rudely at Mohammed's door, and exhorting believers against distrust and uncharitableness among themselves. Sura 9 treats of the campaign to Tebuk (A. H. 9). It opens with the "release" promulgated at the pilgrimage of the same year and declares the antagonism of Islam to all other religions. All but Muslims are excluded from Mecca and the rites of pilgrimage. Idolaters are threatened with slaughter and slavery. War is declared against Jews and Christians until they are humbled and pay tribute. This sura is called "the crusade chapter", and in the early campaigns was often read on the field before battle.

Doctrine

The doctrine of the Koran will be fully discussed in the article on the religion of Islam. It is sufficient to note here that the doctrine may be classified under four categories:

(1) faith, or what to believe; (2) practice or worship; (3) ethics, or what to do and what to avoid; (4) moral, historical, and legendary lessons taken from the canonical, but mostly apocryphal, Christian and Jewish Scriptures, and from contemporary and ancient Arabian heathenism.

Chronological Order and Distinctive Features of the Suras

Various efforts have been made by Muslim writers and European scholars to arrange the suras chronologically, but Nöldeke's arrangement is generally considered the most plausible. He divides the suras into Meccan and

Medinian, namely those delivered at Mecca before the Flight or Hegira, and those delivered at Medina after the Flight. The Meccan suras are divided into three periods. To the first (from the first to the fifth year of Mohammed's mission) belong the following suras — 96, 74, 111, 106, 108, 104, 107, 102, 105, 92, 90, 94, 93, 97, 86, 91, 80, 68, 87, 95, 103, 85, 73, 101, 99, 82, 81, 53, 84, 100, 79, 77, 78, 88, 89, 75, 83, 69, 51, 52, 56, 70, 55, 112, 109, 113, 114, and 1. To the second period (the fifth and sixth year of his mission) are assigned suras 54, 37, 71, 76, 44, 50, 20, 26, 15, 19, 38, 36, 43, 72, 67, 23, 21, 25, 17, 27, and 18. To the third period (from the seventh year to the Flight) belong the following suras: 32, 41 45, 16, 30, 11, 14, 12, 40, 28, 39, 29, 31, 42, 10, 34, 35, 7, 46, 6, and 13. The Medina suras are those which remain, in the following order: 2, 98, 64, 62, 8, 47, 3, 61, 57, 4, 65, 59, 33, 63, 24, 58, 22, 48, 66, 60, 110, 9, and 5.

The characteristic features of the various suras and of the periods in which they were delivered is described by Mr. Palmer as follows:

In the Meccan Suras Mohammed's one and steady purpose is to bring his hearers to a belief in the one only God; this he does by powerful rhetorical displays rather than logical arguments, by appealing to their feelings rather than their

reason; by setting forth the manifestation of God
in His works; by calling nature to witness to His
presence; and by proclaiming His vengeance
against those who associate other gods with Him,
or attribute offsprings to Him. The appeal was
strengthened by glowing pictures of the happiness
in store for those who should believe, and by
frightful descriptions of the everlasting torments
prepared for the unbelievers. In the earlier
chapters, too, the prophetic inspiration the earnest
conviction of the truth of his mission, and the
violent emotion which his sense of responsibility
caused him are plainly shown. The style is curt,
grand, and often almost sublime; the expressions
are full of poetical feeling, and the thoughts are
earnest and passionate, though sometimes dim
and confused, indicating the mental excitement
and doubt through which they struggled to light.

In the second period of the Meccan Suras,
Mohammed appears to have conceived the idea of
still further severing himself from the idolatry of
his compatriots, and of giving to the supreme
deity Allâh another title, Ar-Rahmân, "the merciful
one". The Meccans, however, seem to have taken
these for the names of separate deities, and the
name is abandoned in the later chapters.

In the Suras of the second Meccan period we

first find the long stories of the prophets of olden times, especial stress being laid upon the punishment which fell upon their contemporaries for disbelief; the moral is always the same, namely, that Mohammed came under precisely similar circumstances, and that a denial of the truth of his mission would bring on his fellow-citizens the self-same retribution. They also show the transition stage between the intense and poetical enthusiasm of the early Meccan chapters and the calm teaching of the later Medinah ones. This change is gradual, and even in the later and most prosaic we find occasionally passages in which the old prophetic fire flashes out once more. The three periods are again marked by the oaths which occur throughout the Koran. In the first period they are all frequent and often long, the whole powers of nature being invoked to bear witness to the unity of God and the mission of His Apostle; in the second period they are shorter and of rarer occurrence; in the last period they are absent altogether.

To understand the Medinah Suras we must bear in mind Mohammed's position with respect to the various parties in that city. In Mecca he had been a prophet with little honour in his own country, looked on by some as a madman, and by others as an impostor, both equally grievous to him, while his following consisted of the poorest and meanest of his fellow townsmen. His own clansmen, for the reason that they were his clansmen and for no other, resented the affronts against him. In Medinah he appears as a military leader and a prince, though as yet possessing far from absolute authority. Around in the city were, first, the true believers who had fled with him, El Muhagerin; next, the inhabitants of Yathrib, who had joined him and who were called El Ansar, "the helpers"; and lastly, a large class who are spoken of by the uncomplimentary name of Munafiqun or "hypocrites", consisting of those who went over to his side from fear or compulsion, and lastly those "in whose heart is sickness", who, though believing in him, were prevented by tribal or family ties from going over to him openly. Abdallâh ibn Ubai was a chief whose influence operated strongly against Mohammed, and the latter was obliged to treat him for a long time almost as an equal, even after he had lost his political power. The other party at Medinah was composed of the Jewish tribes settled in and around the city of Yathrib. The Jews were at first looked to as the most natural and likely supporters of the new religion, which was to eboreore inx

Moslemsgment>

confirm their own. These various parties together with the pagan Arabs of Mecca and the Christians are the persons with whom the Medinah Suras chiefly deal. The style of the Medinah Suras resembles that of the third period of the Meccan revelations, the more matter-of-fact nature of the incidents related or the precepts given accounting in a great measure for the more prosaic language in which they are expressed. In the Medinah Suras the prophet is no longer trying to convert his hearers by examples, promises, and warnings; he addresses them as their prince in general, praising them or blaming them for their conduct, and giving them laws and precepts as occasion required. ("The Qur'ân" in "Sacred Books of the East", I, Oxford, 1880, pp. LXI, LXII, and LXIII).

Sources

The sources of the Koran can be reduced to six:

(1) The Old Testament (canonical and apocryphal) and the hybrid Judaism of the late rabbinical schools. During Mohammed's time the Jews were numerous in many parts of Arabia, especially around Medina. Familiarity with them is undoubtly responsible for many Old Testament stories alluded to in the Koran.

52

Later Judaism and Rabbinism are equally well represented (Geiger, "Was hat Mohammed aus dem Judenthum aufgenommen?", Wiesbaden, 1833; tr. "Judaism and Islam", Madras, 1898). (2) The New Testament (canonical and apocryphal) and various heretical doctrines. On his journeys between Syria, Hijaz, and Yemen, Mohammed had every opportunity to come in close touch with Yemenite, Abyssinian, Ghassanide, and Syrian Christians, especially heretic. Hence, while the influence of orthodox Christianity upon the Koran has been slight, apocryphal and heretical Christian legends, on the other hand, are one of the original sources of Koranic faith. (See Muir, op. cit. *infra*, 66-239; Tisdall, "The Original Sources of the Qur'an", London, 1905, 55-211.) (3) Sabaism, a combination of Judaism, Manicheism, and old disfigured Babylonian heathenism. (4) Zoroastrianism. On account of Persia's political influence in the northeastern part of Arabia, it is natural to find Zoroastrian elements in the Koran. (5) Hanifism, the adherents of which, called Hanifs, must have been considerable in number and influence, as it is known from contemporary Arabian sources that twelve of Mohammed's followers were members of this sect. (6) Native ancient and contemporary Arabian heathen beliefs and practices. Wellhausen has collected in his "Reste des arabischen Heidentums" (Berlin, 1897) all that is known of pre-Islamic Arabian heathen belief, traditions, customs, and superstitions, many of which are either alluded to or accepted and incorporated in the Koran. From the various sects and creeds, and Abul-Fida, the well-known historian and geographer of the twelfth century, it is clear that religious beliefs and practices of the Arabs of Mohammed's day form one of the many sources of Islam. From this heathen source Islam derived the practices of polygamy and slavery, which Mohammed sanctioned by adopting them.

Authorship, Compilation

It is generally admitted that the Koran is substantially the work of Mohammed. According to the traditionalists, it contains the pure revelation of God, its primary Author. Mohammed, the Koran tells us, was inspired by the Holy Ghost, Whom he held to be an angel, and Whom he called, in later chapters, written at Medina, by the name of the Archangel Gabriel.

Opinions vary as to Mohammed's ability to read and write. Some traditionalists maintain that prior to the Divine revelation he could neither read nor write, but that immediately afterwards he could do both; others believe that even before the revelation he could read and write; while others, again, deny that he could ever do so. Thus it is uncertain whether any of the suras were written down by the Prophet himself or all delivered by him orally and afterwards written down by others from memory.

The Koran is written in Arabic, in rhymed prose, the style differing considerably in the various suras, according to the various periods of the Prophet's life. The language is universally acknowledged to be the most perfect form of Arab speech, and soon became the standard by which other Arabic literary compositions had to be judged, grammarians, lexicographers, and rhetoricians presuming that the Koran, being the word of God, could not be wrong or imperfect.

Mohammed's hearers began by trusting their memories to retain the words of the revelation they had received from him. Later, those who could write traced them in ancient characters on palm leaves, tanned hides, or dry bones. After the Prophet's death all these fragments were collected. Zaid ibn Thabit, Mohammed's disciple, was charged by Abu-Bekr, the first caliph, to collect all that could be discovered of the sacred text in one volume. The chapters were then arranged according to their length and without regard to historical sequence. The revision made twenty years later affected details of language and grammar rather than the arrangement of the text.

The best and most accessible edition of the Koran is that of Flugel, "Al-Qoran: Corani textus Arabicus"

(Leipzig, 1834 and since). Maracci's famous Latin translation of the Koran, with a refutation and commentary, is still unique and useful: "Alcorani textus universus" (Padua, 1698). The standard English versions are those of Sale (London, 1734) with a still useful introductory essay; Rodwel (London, 1861), arranged in chronological order; and Palmer in "Sacred Books of the East" (Oxford, 1880).

GABRIEL OUSSANI

Christianity in Arabia

The origin and progress of Christianity in Arabia is, owing to the lack of sufficiently authenticated historical documents, involved in impenetrable obscurity, and only detached episodes in one part or another of the peninsula can be grouped together and studied. References to various Christian missionary enterprises in the north and south of the country, found in early ecclesiastical historians and Fathers, such as Eusebius, Rufinus, Socrates, Nicephorus, Metaphrastes, Theodoret, Origen, and Jerome, are valuable, but to be used with caution, inasmuch as a lamentable confusion, common to all writers of that time between Arabia proper and India, or Abyssinia, seems to have crept into their writings.

Furthermore, no proper discrimination is made by any of them among the various traditions at their disposal. More abundant and trustworthy information may be gathered from Nestorian and Jacobite writers, as each of these sects has had its own sphere of influence in the peninsula, and particularly in the northern kingdoms of Hira and Ghassan. Arabic historians (all of post-Islamic times) are very interesting in their allusions to the same, but are at variance with one another. Indigenous ecclesiastical literature and monuments, except perhaps one inscription of the fifth century after Christ found by Glaser, and the ruins of a supposed church, afterwards turned into a heathen temple, are utterly wanting. Christianity in Arabia had three main centres in the north-west, north-east, and south-west of the peninsula. The first embraces the Kingdom of Ghassan (under Roman rule), the second that of Hira (under Persian power), and the third the kingdoms of Himyar, Yemen, and Najran (under Abyssinian rule). As to central and south-east Arabia, such as Nejd and Oman, it is doubtful whether Christianity made any advance there.

North-Arabian Christianity

According to the majority of the Fathers and historians of the Church, the origin of Christianity in northern Arabia is to be traced back to the Apostle Paul, who in his Epistle to the Galatians, speaking of the period of time immediately following his conversion, says: "Neither went I up to Jerusalem to them which were apostles before me; but I went to Arabia, and returned to Damascus" (Gal. i, 17). What particular region of Arabia was visited by the Apostle, the length of his stay, the motive of his journey, the route followed, and the things he accomplished there are not specified. His journey may have lasted as long as one year, and the place visited may have been either the country of the Nabatæans or the Sinaitic peninsula, or better, as Harnack remarks, "not to the desert, but rather to a district south of Damascus where he could not expect to come across any Jews" (*Expansion of Christianity*, 1905, II, 301). Jerome, however, suggests that he may have gone to a tribe where his mission was unsuccessful as regards visible results. Zwemer's suggestion [*Arabia, the Cradle of Islam* (1900), 302- 303] that the Koranic allusion to a certain Nebi Salih, or the Prophet Salih, who is said to have come to the Arabs preaching the truth and was not listened to, and who, consequently, in leaving them said: "O my people, I did preach unto you the message of my Lord, and I gave you good advice, but ye love not sincere advisers" (Surah vii), refers to Paul of Tarsus — this theory need hardly be considered.

In the light of the legend of Abgar of Edessa, however, and considering the fact that the regions lying to the north-west and north-east of Arabia, under Roman and Persian rule respectively, were in constant contact with the northern Arabs, among whom Christianity had already made fast and steady progress, we may reasonably assume that Christian missionary activity cannot have neglected the attractive mission field of northern Arabia. In the Acts of the Apostles (ii, 11) we even read of the presence of Arabians on the day of Pentecost, and Arabs were quite numerous in the Parthian Empire and around Edessa. The cruel persecutions, furthermore, which raged in the Roman and Persian Empires against the followers of Christ must have forced many of these to seek refuge on the safer soil of northern Arabia.

Christianity in Ghassan and North-West Arabia

The Kingdom of Ghassan, in north-western Arabia, adjacent to Syria, comprised a very extensive tract of territory and a great number of Arab tribes whose first migrations there must have taken place as early as the time of Alexander the Great. Towards the third and fourth centuries of the Christian era these tribes already formed a confederation powerful enough to cause trouble to the Roman Empire, which formed with them alliances and friendships in order to counterbalance the influence of the Mesopotamian Arabs of Hira, who were under Persian rule. The kings of Ghassan trace their descent from the tribe of Azd, in Yemen. Gafahah, their first king, dispossessed the original dynasty, and is said to have been confirmed in his conquest by the Roman governor of Syria. Their capital city was Balka

till the time of the second Hârith, when it was
supplanted by Petra and Sideir. Although living a
nomadic life and practically independent, with "no
dwelling but the tent, no intrenchment but the sword,
no law but the traditional song of their bards," these
Arabs were under the nominal, but quite effective,
control of the Romans as early as the time of Pompey.
Such Syrian Arabs always looked upon the Romans as
their best and most powerful defenders and protectors
against the Sassanian dynasty of Persia, by which they
were constantly oppressed and molested.

The Nabatæan Kingdom, which comprised the
Sinaitic peninsula, the sea-coast to the Gulf of Akaba,
to Al-Haura, and as far as Damascus and Hijaz, and
which was annexed to the Roman Empire in A.D. 105,
comprised also many Arab tribes which were for a long
time governed by their own sheikhs and princes, their
stronghold being the country around Bosra and
Damascus. These sheikhs were acknowledged as such
by the Roman emperors who gave them the title of
phylarch. The ever increasing number and importance
of these tribes and of those living in the Ghassanide
territory were such that in 531, by the consent and
authority of the Emperor Justinian, a real Arab-Roman
kingdom was formed under the rule of the kings of
Ghassan, whose power and authority extended over all
the Arabs of Syria, Palestine, Phœnicia and north-

western Arabia. Another Syro-Arabian Kingdom, in which Arab tribes were very numerous, is that of Palmyra, which retained for a long time its independence and resisted all encroachments. Under Odenathus the Palmyrene kingdom flourished, and it reached the zenith of its power under his wife and successor, the celebrated Zenobia. After her defeat by Aurelian (272), Palmyra and its dependencies became a province of the Roman Empire.

Christianity must have been introduced among the Syrian Arabs at a very early period; if not among the tribes living in the interior of the Syro-Arabian desert, certainly among those whose proximity brought them into continuous social and commercial contact with Syria. Rufinus (*Hist. Ecclesiastica*, II, 6) tells us of a certain Arabian Queen, Mavia, or Maowvia (better, Mu'awiyah), who, after having repeatedly fought against the Romans, accepted peace on condition that a certain monk, called Moses, should be appointed bishop over her tribe. This took place during the reign of Valens (about 374), who was greatly inclined to Arianism. Moses lived a hermit life in the desert of Egypt, and accordingly he was brought to Alexandria in order to be ordained bishop, as the Bedouin queen required. The Bishop of Alexandria was then a certain Lucius, accused of Arianism. Moses refused to be ordained by a heretical bishop, and was so obdurate in his refusal that it was necessary for the emperor to bring from exile a Catholic bishop and send him to the queen.

Caussin de Perceval (*Histoire des Arabes avant l'Islamisme*, etc., II, 215) affirms that towards the beginning of the fourth century, and during the reign of Djabala I, Christianity was again preached, and accepted by another Arab tribe. Sozomenus, in fact, relates that before the time of Valens an Arab prince, whom he calls Zacome, or Zocum, having obtained a son through the prayers of a Syrian hermit, embraced Christianity, and all his tribe with him. Le Quien (*Oriens Christianus*, II, 851) calls this prince Zaracome and places him under the reign of Constantine or of one of his sons. No prince of such name, however, occurs in any Arabic historian, although Caussin de Perceval suggests his identification with a certain Arcan, of the tribe of Giafnah, who was in all probability a prominent chief of Ghassan.

Another source of Christian propaganda among the northern Arabs was undoubtedly the many holy hermits and monks scattered in the Syro-Arabian desert, for whom the Arab tribes had great respect, and to whose solitary abodes they made numerous pilgrimages. Jerome and Theodoret explicitly affirm that the life and miracles of St. Hilarion and of St. Simeon the Stylite made a deep impression on the

Bedouin Arabs. Many tribes accepted Christianity at the hands of the latter Saint, while many others became so favourably disposed towards it that they were baptized by the priests and bishops of Syria. Cyrillus of Scythopolis (sixth century), in his life of Saint Euthymius, the monk of Pharan, tells the story of the conversion of an entire Arab tribe which, towards 420, had migrated from along the Euphrates into Palestine. Their chief was a certain Aspebætos. He had a son afflicted with paralysis, who at the prayers of the saint completely recovered. Aspebætos himself was afterwards ordained bishop over his own tribe by the Patriarch of Jerusalem (see below). These detached facts clearly indicate that during the fourth, fifth, and sixth centuries of the Christian Era, Christianity must have been embraced by many Arabs, and especially by the tribe of Ghassan, which is celebrated by Arab historians and poets as being from very early times devotedly attached to Christianity. It was of this tribe that the proverb became current: "They were lords in the days of ignorance [i.e., before Mohammed] and stars of Islam." (Zwemer, *Arabia, the Cradle of Islam*, 304.)

The numerous inscriptions collected in northern Syria by Waddington, de Voguë, Clermont Ganneau, and others also clearly indicate the presence of Christian elements in the Syro-Arabian population of that region and especially around Bosra. In the days of Origen there were numerous bishoprics in the towns lying south of the Hauran, and these bishops were once grouped together in a single synod (Harnack, *Expansion of Christianity*, II, 301). As early as the third century this part of Syro-Arabia was already well known as the "mother of heresies." Towards the year 244 Origen converted to the orthodox faith Beryllus, Bishop of Bosra, who was a confessed anti-Trinitarian (Eusebius, *Hist. Eccl.*, VI, 20); and two years earlier (242) a provincial synod of Arabia was held in connection with the proceedings against Origen, which decided in his favour. This great teacher in the Church was also personally known at that time to the Arabian bishops; for about the year 215 he had travelled as far as Arabia at the request of the Roman governor, before whom he laid his views (Eusebius, op. cit., VI, 19, and Harnack, op. cit., 301). In 250 the same teacher went to Arabia for the second time to combat certain heretics who taught that the soul died with the body, but that it would rise up again with it on the Judgment Day (Eusebius, op. cit., VI, 39).

The "Onomasticon" of Eusebius and the Acts of the Council of Nicæa (325) also indicate the presence of Christians, during the days of Eusebius, in Arabia, along the Dead Sea, and around Qariathaim, near Madaba (Harnack, op. cit., 302-303). At the Council of

Nicæa there were present six bishops of the province of Arabia: the Bishops of Bosra, Philadelphia, Jabrudi, Sodom, Betharma, and Dionysias (Wright, *Early Christianity in Arabia*, 73, and Harnack, op. cit., 303). One tradition makes an Arabian bishop of Zanaatha (Sanaa?) attend Nicaea. The sheikh-bishop Aspebætos was present at the Council of Ephesus (431), and one of his successors, Valens by name, became, in 518, a suffragan bishop of the Patriarchate of Jerusalem (Duchesne, *Les églises séparées*, 343). A certain Eustathius, called "Bishop of the Sarrasins," assisted at the Council of Chalcedon. In 458 he was still Bishop of Damascus. At the second Council of Ephesus (449) there was present another bishop of the "allied Arabs," named Auxilaos. Another Arabian bishopric was that of the island of Jotabe, near the Gulf of Akabah; and a Bishop of Jotabe, by the name of Anastasius was present at the Council of Jerusalem (536). At the First and Second Councils of Constantinople, we read of the presence of the Metropolitan of Bosra, whose authority is said to have extended over twenty churches or bishoprics (Assemani, *Bibliotheca Orientalis*, III, Part II, 598 sqq.). Many of these Arabian bishops were undoubtedly infected with Arianism, and later on with Monophysitism, the latter sect having been greatly favoured and even protected by the Ghassanide princes.

The above sketch clearly shows that Christian Arab tribes were scattered through all Syria, Phoenicia, and northern Arabia, having their own bishops and churches. But it is doubtful whether this North-Arabian Christianity formed any national Church, as many of their bishops were dependent on the Greek Metropolitans of Tyrus, Jerusalem, Damascus, and on the Patriarchs of Jerusalem and Antioch.

Christianity in Hira and North-East Arabia

According to Arabic writers and historians, the first Arab migration into Hira took place about A.D. 192 by the tribe of Tenukh and under the leadership of its chief, Malik ibn Fahm. This tribe was shortly afterwards followed by other tribes, such as those of Iyad, Azd, Qudâ'ah, and others, most of whom settled around Anb'âr, and who afterwards built for themselves the city of Hira, not far from the modern Kufa on the Euphrates, in southern Babylonia. We know, however, that as early as the time of Alexander, and towards the first century of the Christian Era, northern and southern Mesopotamia were thickly inhabited by Arab tribes, who, about the third century, formed more than one-third of its population. These tribes were, of course, governed by their own chiefs and princes, subject, however, to Persia.

Tradition relates that under one of these princes of Hira, Imru'ul Qais I, who reigned from 288 to 338, Christianity was first introduced into Hira and among the Mesopotamian Arabs. This, however, is not correct, for, from the Syriac Acts of the Apostles Addai and Mari, and other Syriac documents, we know that Christianity was introduced into Mesopotamia and Babylonia, if not at the end of the first, certainly towards the middle of the second century. The Acts of the Persian martyrs and the history of the Christian Church of Persia and Madâin (i.e., Seleucia and Ctesiphon) unmistakably show that Christianity, although fiercely persecuted and opposed by the Sassanian kings of Persia, made rapid progress in these and the neighbouring regions, and, consequently, the Arabs of Hira cannot have entirely missed the beneficial effects of the new religion. We know also that during the reign of Hormuz I (271-273) several hundred Christian captives were brought from Syria and other Roman provinces into Irak and Babylonia. According to Tabari (ed. Nöldeke, 24), the Christians of Hira were called *'Ibâd*, or "Worshippers", i.e., "worshippers of God", in opposition to "pagans" (Labourt, *Le Christianisme dans l'empire perse sous la dynastie sassanide*, 1904, 206).

The condition of the Christian Church in Persia and Mesopotamia in the early centuries is well known to us from the numerous Acts of martyrs and other Syriac documents still extant, but that of the Christian Arabs of Hira is very obscure. We know, however, that towards the end of the fourth and the beginning of the fifth century, Christianity attained there considerable success and popularity. Nu'mân I, King of Hira, who reigned from 390 to 418, is said to have been, if not a follower of Christ, certainly a great protector of his Christian subjects. During his reign the Kingdom of Hira rose to great power and celebrity, for his domain extended over all the Arabs of Mesopotamia, over Babylonia, along the Euphrates down to the Persian Gulf, and as far south as the islands of Bahrein. He caused great and magnificent buildings to be erected, among which were the two famous castles of Khawarnig and Sidir, celebrated in Arabic poetry for their unsurpassed splendour and beauty. The city of Hira was then, as afterwards, called after his own name, i.e., "the Hira of Nu'mân", or "the city of Nu'mân", and his deeds and exploits are justly celebrated by Arab writers, historians, and poets. Before and during the reign of this prince, the Persian monarchs, from Shapor to Kobad, had relentlessly persecuted the Christians, and their hatred for the new religion was naturally imparted to their vassal kings and allies, principal among whom was Nu'mân.

In 410 St. Simeon the Stylite, who was in all

probability of Arab descent, retired to the Syro-Arabian desert. There the fame of his sanctity and miracles attracted a great many pilgrims from all Syria, Mesopotamia, and northern Arabia, many of whom were Nu'mân's subjects. The pious example and eloquent exhortations of the Syrian hermit induced many of these heathen Arabs to embrace Christianity, and Nu'mân began to fear lest his Christian subjects might be led by their religion to desert to the service of the Romans. Accordingly, he forbade all pilgrimages to the Syrian saint and all intercourse with the Christian Romans, under penalty of instant death. On the night of the issue of the edict, St. Simeon is said to have appeared to him in a dream, threatening him with death if he did not revoke the edict and allow his Christian subjects absolute religious freedom. Terrified and humbled, Nu'mân revoked the order and became himself a sincere admirer of Christianity, which his fear of the Persian king did not permit him to embrace. When the change of sentiment that had taken place in their prince was publicly known, the Arabs of his kingdom are said to have flocked in crowds to receive the Christian faith. This memorable event seems to all appearances, to be historical; for it is related by Cosmas the Presbyter, who assures us that he heard it personally from a certain Roman general, Antiochus by name, to whom it was narrated by Nu'mân himself

(Assemani, *Bibliotheca Orientalis*, I, 247; and Wright, op. cit., 77). Hamza, Abul-Faraj of Isfahan (the author of Kitab-al-Aghâni), Abulfeda, Nuwairi, Tabari, and Ibn Khaldun (quoted by Caussin de Perceval, *Histoire des Arabes*, etc., III, 234) relate that Nu'mân abdicated the throne and retired to a religious and ascetic life, although he is nowhere expressly said to have become a Christian. (See also J.E. Assemani, *Acta Martyrum Orientalium*, II, and *Bibl. Orient.*, I, 276-278.)

The greatest obstacle to the spread and success of Christianity in Hira was the immoderate hatred of the Sassanian monarchs towards the Christians of their empire and the fierce persecutions to which these were subjected. Encouraged and incited by these suzerains, the princes of Hira persecuted more than once their Christian subjects, destroyed their churches, and sentenced to death their bishops, priests, and consecrated virgins. One of these Princes, Mundhir ibn Imru'ul-Qais, to whom Dhu Nuwas sent the news of the massacre of the Christians of Najran, in southern Arabia, sacrificed at the altar of the goddess Ouzza, the Arabian Venus, four hundred venerated Christian virgins (Tabari, ed. Nöldeke, 171). His wife, however, was a fervent Christian of the royal family of Ghassan, Hind by name. She founded at Hira a famous monastery after her own name, in which many Nestorian patriarchs and bishops resided and were buried. Yaqut, in his "Geographical Dictionary" (ed. Wüstenfeld) reproduces the dedicatory inscription which was placed at the entrance of the church. It runs as follows: "This church was built by Hind, the daughter of Harith ibn Amr ibn Hujr, the queen daughter of Kings, the mother of King Amr ibn Mundhir, the servant of Christ, the mother of His servant and the daughter of His servants [i.e., her son and her ancestors, the Christian kings of Ghassan], under the reign of the King of Kings, Khosroë Anoushirwan, in the times of Bishop Mar Ephrem. May God, to Whose honour she built this church, forgive her sins, and have mercy on her and on her son. May He accept him and admit him into His abode of peace and truth. That He may be with her and with her son in the centuries to come." (See Duchesne, *Les églises séparées*, 350-351.)

The inscription was written during the reign of her Christian son, Amr ibn Mundhir, who reigned after his idolatrous father, from 554 to 569. After him reigned his brother Nu'mân ibn Qabus. This prince is said to have been led to embrace Christianity by his admiration of the constancy and punctuality of a Christian Syrian whom he had designed to put to death. "In a fit of drunkenness he had wantonly killed two of his friends, and when sober, in repentance for his cruelty and in remembrance of their friendship, he erected tombs over their graves, and vowed to moisten them once every year with the blood of an enemy. One of the first victims intended for the fulfilment of his vow was this Christian of Syria, who entreated the Mundhir to allow him a short space of time to return home for the purpose of acquitting himself of some duty with which he had been entrusted; the boon was granted on his solemn promise to return at an appointed time. The time came and the Christian Syrian was punctual to his word, and thus saved his life." (Wright, op. cit. 143, from Pococke, "Specimen Historiæ Arabum," 75). After his conversion to Christianity, Qabus melted down a statue of Venus of solid gold, which had been worshipped by his tribe, and distributed its gold produce among the poor (Evagrius, *Hist. Eccl.*, VI, xxii). Following his example, many Arabs became Christians and were baptized.

Qabus was succeeded by his brother, Mundhir ibn Mundhir, during whose reign paganism held sway once more among his subjects, and Christianity was kept in check. After him reigned Nu'mân ibn Mundhir (580-595), who, towards the year 594, was converted to Christianity. His granddaughter, Hind, who was a Christian and of exceptional beauty, was married to the Arab poet 'Adi ibn Zayd. He saw her for the first time during a Palm Sunday procession in the church of Hira, and became infatuated with her. Nu'mân was one of the last kings of his dynasty that reigned at Hira. One of his sons, Mundhir ibn Nu'mân, lived in the time of Mohammed, whom he opposed at the head of a Christian Arab army of Bahrein; but he fell in battle, in 633, while fighting the invading Moslem army.

The Christians of Hira professed both the Nestorian and the Monophysite heresies; both sects having had their own bishops, churches, and monasteries within the same city. Bishops of Hira (in Syriac, *Hirtha de Tayyaye*, or "Hira of the Arabs") are mentioned as present at the various councils held in 410, 430, 485, 499, and 588. Towards the year 730 the Diocese of Hira was subdivided into three dioceses with three distinct bishops bearing the respective titles of Bishop of Akula, Bishop of Kufa and Bishop of the Arabs, or of the tribe of Ta'lab. From 686-724, Georgius, the famous Bishop of the Arabs, was still entitled Bishop of the Tanukhites, of the Tayyaites, and of the Akulites, i.e., of the tribe of Tanoukh, of Tay, and of the district of Akula [Assemani, *Bibl. Orient.*, II, 459, 419; Lequien, *Oriens Christianus*, II, 1567, 1585, and 1597; Guidi, *Zeitschrift für deutsche morgenländische Gesellschaft*, XLIII, 410; Ryssel, *Georgs des Araberbischofs Gedichte und Briefe*, 44; Duchesne, op. cit., 349-352; Chabot, *Synodicon Orientale* (1902), 275; Labourt, *Le Christianisme dans l'empire Perse sous la dynastie Sassanide* (1904), 206-207, 158, and passim].

South-Arabian Christianity:
Himyar, Yemen and Najran

According to Eusebius, Rufinus, Nicephorus, Theodoret, etc., followed by Baronius, Assemani, Tillemont, Lequien, Pagi, and others, the Apostle Bartholomew, while on his way to India (i.e., Ethiopia), preached the Gospel in Arabia Felix, or Yemen, which was then, especially after the expedition of Ælius Gallus, a commercial country well known to the Romans, and in constant mercantile and political communication with Abyssinia. Eusebius informs us that in the second century Pantænus, master of the school of Alexandria, instructed the Indians (Ethiopians) in Christianity, and Jerome adds further that this missionary was sent to them by Demetrius, Bishop of Alexandria, in consequence of a request made by them for a Christian teacher. As the names India and Indians were applied by the Greek and Latin writers indiscriminately to Parthia, Persia, Media, Ethiopia, Libya, and Arabia, it may be reasonably inferred that the tradition in question is at the least vague and indefinite, although it is universally admitted that the India in question is Ethiopia, whence the Apostle may have easily crossed to Yemen; inasmuch as the Ethiopians and the Himyarites, or Yemenites, are both linguistically and ethnographically the same race.

According to Nicephorus, the field of Pantænus's mission was among the Jews of Yemen, whom we know to have settled in various centres of southern Arabia after the ruin of the second Temple in order to escape the Roman persecution. Jerome adds, furthermore, that Pantænus found among them the Hebrew Gospel of St. Matthew which they had received from their first Apostle, St. Bartholomew. Rufinus, Theodoret, and Eusebius assert that during the reign of Constantine the Great (312-337) a Tyrian philosopher named Meropius determined to visit the Himyarites in Arabia Felix. He was accompanied by two of his kinsmen (according to some, his two sons) and other disciples. On their return they were captured as enemies and were either slain or made captives, for at that time the Himyarites were in a state of warfare. Two members of the party, however, named Ædesius and Frumentius respectively, were taken before the King of Himyar, who became favourably disposed towards them, appointing the first his cup-bearer, the other custodian of his treasures. At the death of the king, the two Christian Tyrians determined to return to their country, but were prevented by the queen regent, who requested them to remain and be the guardians of her infant son till he reached the proper age. They obeyed, and Frumentius, taking advantage of his power and position, caused a search to be made for the few

Christians who, he had heard, were scattered in the
Himyarite Kingdom. He treated them kindly and built
for them churches and places of worship.

As soon as the young king ascended the throne, the
two disciples returned to Tyre, where Aedesius was
ordained priest. Frumentius went to Alexandria to
inform the newly-elected bishop, Athanasius, of the
condition of Christianity in Himyar, and begged him to
send them a bishop and priests. Whereupon
Frumentius himself was consecrated bishop and sent,
together with several priests, to the Himyarites where,
with the aid and favour of the king, he increased the
number of Christians and brought much prosperity to
the Church. As Duchesne remarks ["Les églises
séparées" (1905), 311], the elevation of Frumentius
must have taken place during the reign of Constantius,
and either shortly before 340, or shortly after 346; for
during the interval Athanasius was absent from
Alexandria, and, as the stay of the two Tyrians at the
court of Himyar cannot have lasted less than fifteen
years, it follows that Meropius's journey must have
taken place between the years 320 and 325. The legend
of Meropius and Frumentius, however, seems to refer
to the evangelization of Ethiopia rather than to that of
Himyar, or, if to that of Himyar, its conversion must
have been only of an indirect and transitory character.
To the mission of Frumentius may also refer the

testimony of two Arabic writers quoted by Ouseley (*Travels*, I, 369-371; also Wright, *Christianity in Arabia*, 33), according to which the Arabs of Najran in Yemen, were first converted by a Syrian Christian captured by some Arab robbers and taken to their country.

Another Christian mission to Himyar took place during the reign of Constantius (337-361), who towards the year 356, chose Bishop Theophilus, the famous deacon of Nicomedia and a zealous Arian, to conduct an embassy to the court of Himyar. The eloquence of Theophilus so impressed the king that he became favourably disposed towards the Christians of his realm and built three churches for them, one at Dhafar (or Safar), another at Aden or at Sanaa, and the third at Hormuz, near the Persian Gulf. As the aim of the embassy was to ask the King of Himyar to grant freedom of worship to the Roman citizens in the Kingdom of Himyar, it follows that Christianity must have attained there a certain importance. According to Philostorgius, the king himself became a Christian, but this is improbable. At any rate, whether Theophilus succeeded in converting more Himyarites to the Christian faith or whether, as Assemani seems to believe, he simply perverted the already existing Christian population to the Arian heresy cannot be determined. From the fact that the latest royal Himyarite inscription, couched in pagan terms, bears the date of 281, that local Jewish inscriptions date from 378, 448, 458, and 467, and that the first Christian inscription, discovered by Glaser and considered by Hommel the latest Sabean inscription (it opens with the words: "In the power of the All-Merciful, and His Messiah and the Holy Ghost"), dates only as late as 542-543 [Glaser, *Skizze der Geschichte Arabiens* (1889), 12 sqq.], it does not follow that Christianity at the time of Theophilus had not attained any official position in Himyar, although it is undeniable that the two prevailing creeds were then Paganism and Judaism. Arab historians, such as Ibn Khallikan, Yaqut, Abulfeda, Ibn-al-Athir and especially the early biographers of Mohammed, unanimously affirm that towards the fourth and fifth centuries of the Christian Era Christianity flourished in Hira, Himyar, and Najran, and among many tribes of the North and South, Quda'ah, Bahrah, Tanukh, Taghlib, Tay. We are far, however, from accepting all these ecclesiastical testimonies concerning the origin and development of Christianity in South Arabia as critically ascertained and conclusive. Fictitious elements and legendary traditions are undoubtedly ingredients of the original narratives, yet it cannot be doubted that a certain amount of truth is contained in them.

Positive traces of ecclesiastical organization in southern Arabia first appear in the time of the Emperor

Anastasius (491-518). John Diacrinomenos (P.G., LXXXVI, 212) relates that during this emperor's reign the Himyarites, who had become followers of Judaism since the time of the Queen of Sheba, or Saba, were converted to Christianity, and received a bishop, Silvanus by name, who was that writer's own uncle, and at whose instance he wrote his ecclesiastical history. It is not improbable that the testimony of Ibn Ishaq, the earliest and most authoritative biographer of Mohammed (d. 770), according to which the first apostle of Christianity in Yemen was a poor Syrian mason named Phemion, who with a companion named Salih was captured by an Arab caravan and sold to a prominent Najranite, refers to this Silvanus. One of his first converts was a certain Abdallah ibn Thamir, who became a great miracle-worker and thus succeeded in converting the town of Najran to the religion of Christ (Tabari, ed. Nöldeke, 178). According to Halévy (*Archives des missions*, VII, 40), even at the present time there is still a mosque in Najran dedicated to this Abdallah ibn Thamir. Ibn Khaldun, on the other hand, asserts that as early as the latter half of the third century, a certain Abd-Kelal, son of Dhu-l Awad, who was King of Himyar and Yemen from 273 to 297, became a Christian through the teaching of a Syrian monk, but, on being discovered by his people, was killed (Caussin de Perceval, *Histoire des Arabes avant l'Islamisme*, III, 234). Assemani, followed by Caussin de Perceval, thinks that Christianity first entered Najran in the time of Dhu Nuwas (sixth century). This king, he says, was so alarmed by its advance that he ordered a general massacre of the Christians if they refused to embrace Judaism, to which he and his whole dynasty belonged. He identifies Harith, or Arethas, the Christian prince and martyr of Najran, with the above-mentioned Abdallah ibn Thamir, whose tribe's name was, according to him, Harith or Arethas. This, however, is improbable, for at the time of Dhu Nuwas's accession to the throne, Christianity was already flourishing at Najran, with its own bishop, priests, and churches.

What was the exact condition of Christianity in southern Arabia during the fifth and sixth centuries, we do not know; but from the episode of the martyrs of Najran it clearly appears that its spread was constant and steady. The principal and most powerful obstacle to the permanent success of Christianity in Yemen was undoubtedly the numerous communities of Jews scattered in that section of the peninsula, who had acquired so great a religious, political, and monetary influence that they threatened for a while to become the dominant power. They had their own poets and orators, synagogues, schools, princes and even kings. Their power was constantly used to keep in check the progress of Christianity, and they were the direct cause of the almost entire annihilation of the Christians of Najran. "Like other religious communities which preach toleration when oppressed, they [the Arab Jews] became persecutors when they had acquired sovereignty." —Margoliouth, *Mohammed and the Rise of Islam* (London, 1905), 36. This persecution, which occurred in 523, and in which the Jews piled faggots and lit fires, and the Christians were burned, happened as follows.

About the beginning of the sixth century, the Kingdom of Himyar and Yemen was subject to Abyssinian rule. Kalib, King of Abyssinia, known by the Greek historians under the name of Elesbaan, or Hellesthaios, had succeeded, after a desperate struggle, in subjugating Himyar to the throne of Ethiopia. Though not a Christian, he was favourably inclined towards Christianity, as he was on friendly terms with the Romans. He is said to have vowed to become a Christian in the event of his conquering Himyar, a vow he in all probability fulfilled. Rabiah ibn Mudhar, the defeated Himyarite king, who, like all his predecessors of the same dynasty, was a Jew, was compelled to seek shelter in Hira, and was succeeded by a certain Yusuf Dhu Nuwas, likewise a Jew, but a vassal to the Negus of Abyssinia. About the year 523 (not 560, as the majority of Arab historians believe), and as soon as the victorious Abyssinian army had retraced its steps, Dhu Nuwas revolted against Elesbaan and, instigated by the Jews, resolved to wreak his vengeance on the Christians. All who refused to renounce their faith and embrace Judaism were put to death without respect to age or sex. The town of Najran, to the north of Yemen, and the bulwark of South-Arabian Christianity, suffered the most. Dhu Nuwas marched against the latter city and, finding it impregnable, treacherously promised the inhabitants full amnesty in the case of their surrender.

On entering the city, Dhu Nuwas ordered a general massacre of all the Christians. "Large pits were dug in the neighbourhood and filled with burning fuel, and all those who refused to abjure their faith and embrace Judaism, amounting to many thousands, including the priests and monks of the surrounding regions, with the consecrated virgins and the matrons who had retired to lead a monastic life, were committed to the flames. The chief men of the town, with their prince, Arethas [called by some Arabian writers Abdallah ibn Athamir], a man distinguished for his wisdom and piety, were put in chains. Dhu Nuwas next sought their bishop, Paul, and when informed that he had been some time dead, he ordered his bones to be disinterred and burnt and their ashes scattered to the wind. Arethas and his companions were conducted to the side of a small brook in the neighbourhood, where they were beheaded. Their wives, who had shown the same constancy, were afterwards dragged to a similar fate. One named Ruma, the wife of the chief, was brought with her two virgin daughters before Dhu Nuwas; their surpassing beauty is said to have moved his compassion, but their constancy and devotion provoked in a still greater degree his vengeance; the daughters were put to death before the face of their mother, and Ruma, after having been compelled to taste their blood, shared their fate. When he had thus perpetrated the tragedy of Najran, Dhu Nuwas returned with his army to Sanaa." — Wright, op. cit., 54-55.

From here Dhu Nuwas hastened to inform his friends and allies, Kabad, King of Persia, and Al-Mundhir, Prince of Hira, of the event, urging them to imitate his example and exterminate their Christian subjects. Dhu Nuwas's messengers arrived 20 January, 524, at Hufhuf (El-Hassa), near the Persian Gulf, where Al-Mundhir was then entertaining an embassy sent to him by the Emperor Justin and composed of Sergius, Bishop of Rosapha, the priest Abramos, and many other ecclesiastics and laymen, among whom was the Monophysite Simeon, Bishop of Beth-Arsam, in Persia. Al-Mundhir received and communicated the news of the massacre to the members of the embassy, who were horrified. According to Ibn Ishaq, the number of the massacred Christians was 20,000, while the letter of the Bishop of Beth-Arsam said there were 427 priests, deacons, monks, and consecrated virgins, and more than 4,000 laymen. This Monophysite Bishop of Persia, immediately after his return to Hira, wrote a circumstantial account of the sufferings of the Christians of Najran and sent it to Simeon, Abbot of Gabula, near Chalcis. In it he asks to have the news communicated to the Patriarch of Alexandria, to the King of Abyssinia, to the Bishops of Antioch, Tarsus, Cæsarea in Cappadocia, and Edessa, and urges his Roman brethren to pray for the afflicted Najranites and to take up their cause. A certain Dhu Thaleban, who escaped the massacre, fled to the court of Constantinople and implored the emperor to advocate the cause of his persecuted countrymen. In the meanwhile the news of the massacre had spread all over the Roman and Persian Empires; for in that same year John the Psalmist, Abbot of the Monastery of Beth Aphtonios, wrote in Greek an elegy on the Najranite martyrs and their chief, Harith. Bishop Sergius of Rosapha, the head of the embassy, wrote also a very detailed account of the same events in Greek. Even in the Koran (Surah lxxxv) the event is mentioned, and is universally alluded to by all subsequent Arab, Nestorian, Jacobite, and Occidental historians and writers.

The news of the massacre weighed heavily on Elesbaan, King of Abyssinia, who is said to have now become a very fervent Christian. He determined to take revenge on Dhu Nuwas, to avenge the massacre of the Christian Najranites, and to punish the Yemenite Jews. Accordingly, at the head of seventy thousand men and a powerful flotilla, he descended upon Himyar, invaded Yemen, and with relentless fury massacred thousands of Jews. Dhu Nuwas, after a brave fight, was defeated and slain, and his whole army routed. The whole fertile land was once more a scene of bloodshed and devastation. The churches built before the days of Dhu Nuwas were again rebuilt on the sites of their ruins, and new bishops and priests were appointed in the place of the martyrs. An Abyssinian general, Esimephæus, was appointed King of Himyar, and during his reign a certain Dhu Giadan, of the family of Dhu Nuwas, attempted to raise the standard of revolt, but was defeated. A few years later the Himyarites, under the leadership of Abramos, or Abraha, a Christian Abyssinian, revolted against Esimephæus, and in order to put down the revolution the King of Abyssinia sent an army under the command of one of his relatives, Arethas, or Aryat. The latter was slain, however, by his own soldiers who joined the party of Abramos. A second Abyssinian army took the field, but was cut to pieces and destroyed. Abramos became King of Himyar, and from Procopius we know that he, after the death of Elesbaan, made peace with the Emperor of Abyssinia and acknowledged his sovereignty.

During the reign of Abramos Christianity in South Arabia enjoyed great peace and prosperity. "Paying tribute only to the Abyssinian crown, and at peace with all the Arab tribes, Abraha was loved for his justice and moderation by all his subjects and idolized by the Christians for his burning zeal in their religion." Large numbers of Jews were baptized who were said to have been converted to Christianity by a public dispute between them and St. Gregentius, the Arabian Bishop of Dhafar. In this dispute the Jews were represented by Herban, one of their most learned rabbis, and Christ is said to have appeared in Heaven. Many idolaters sought admission to the Church; new schemes of benevolence were inaugurated, and the foundations were being laid for a magnificent cathedral at Sanaa, where is said to have existed a picture of the Madonna, afterwards moved by the Quraishites and placed in the Caaba, at Mecca (Margoliouth, op. cit., 42).

In short, South-Arabian Christianity, during the reign of Abramos, i.e., in the first half of the sixth century, "seemed on the eve of its Golden Age" (Zwemer, *Arabia, the Cradle of Islam*, 308). The king is also said to have framed, with the assistance of Bishop Gregentius, his great friend, admirer and counsellor, a code of laws for the people of Himyar, still extant in Greek, and divided in twenty-three sections. The authenticity of this code, however, is doubted by many, as it is more ascetic and monastic in character than social. The whole career, in fact, of St. Gregentius and his relations with Elesbaan, Abramos, and Herban are interwoven with legend (Duchesne, op. cit., 334-336). In 550, Abramos's glorious reign came to a disastrous end. According to Arab historians, the event took place in 570, the year of Mohammed's birth; but, as Nöldeke has shown, this is simply an ingenious arrangement in order to connect the rise of Islam with the overthrow of the Christian rule in Yemen; for the latter event must have taken place at least twenty years earlier (Tabar, I, 205). Abramos's defeat is reported by all Mohammedan historians with great joy and satisfaction, and is known among them as the "Day of the Elephant." Mohammed himself devoted to it an entire surah of his Koran. This defeat forms the last chapter in the history of South-Arabian Christianity and the preface to the advent of Mohammed and Islam. It was brought about as follows.

Towards the first half of the sixth century the temple of Caaba, in Mecca, had become, as of old, the Eleusis of Arabia. It was sought and annually visited by thousands of Arabs from all parts of the peninsula, and enriched with presents and donations of every kind and description. Its custodians were of the tribe of Quraish, to which Mohammed belonged, and which had then become the most powerful and illustrious one of Hijaz. Abramos, the Christian King of Himyar, beheld with grief the multitudes of pilgrims who went to pay their superstitious devotions to the heathen deities of the Caaba, and, in order to divert the attention and worship of the heathen Arabs to another object, he resolved to build a magnificent church at Sanaa. The edifice was completed, and far surpassed the Caaba in the splendour of its decorations. To attain his object, Abramos issued a proclamation ordering the pilgrims to relinquish their former route for the shorter and more convenient journey to the Christian church of Sanaa. The object was attained, and the Quraish found themselves reduced to a precarious financial and politico-religious condition. To avenge themselves and to depreciate in the eyes of the Arab tribes the Christian church of Sanaa they hired a certain man of the Kenanah tribe to enter the church and defile it by strewing it with dung, which was enough to make the Arabs look at the place with horror and disgust. The desecration was successfully effected, and its criminal agent fled, spreading everywhere in his flight the news of the profanation of the Christian church. The act was a signal of war and vengeance, and Abramos determined to destroy the tribes of Kenanah and

Quraish, and to demolish the Caaba. Accordingly at the head of a powerful army, accompanied by numerous elephants, he invaded Hijaz, defeated the hostile tribes in his way, and approached Mecca.

The chief of the tribe of Quraish and the guardian of the Caaba was then the venerable Abdul-Muttalib ibn Hashim, the grandfather of Mohammed. This chief, at the news of the approach of the Himyarite army, sought peace with Abramos, offering him as a ransom for the Caaba a third part of the wealth of Hijaz; but Abramos was inflexible. Despairing of victory and overwhelmed with terror, the inhabitants of Mecca, led by Abdul-Muttalib, took refuge in the neighbouring mountains that overhung the narrow pass through which the enemy must advance. Approaching the city by way of the narrow valley, Abramos and his army, not knowing that the heights were occupied by the Quraishites, fell beneath the numberless masses of rock and other missiles incessantly poured upon them and their elephants by the assailants. Abramos was defeated and compelled to retreat. His army was almost annihilated, and the king himself returned a fugitive to Sanaa, where he died soon after, as much of vexation as of his wounds.

Mohammedan writers attribute the defeat of Abramos and the victory of Quraish to supernatural intervention, not unlike that which defeated the army of Sennacherib under the walls of Jerusalem. Be this as it may, by the defeat of the Himyarite army Quraish became supreme in command and authority. In the meanwhile, Yaksoum and Masrouq, sons of Abramos, had succeeded him in turn, but their power had so much declined that they had to seek alliance with the Sassanian kings of Persia, which caused a general revolt in southern and central Arabia. In 568, two years before Mohammed's birth, a Persian military expedition invaded Yemen and Oman and brought the Christian Abyssinian dynasty and that of Abramos to an end. A tributary prince was appointed over Himyar by the Sassanian kings, in the person of Saif dhu Yezen, a descendant of the old royal race of Himyar. This prince, during the rein of Masrouq, and at the instigation of some noble and rich Himyarites who had assisted him with money and all the means available, repaired to Constantinople and appealed to Mauricius, the Byzantine emperor, for assistance in delivering Himyar from the Abyssinian yoke. Mauricius refused to help him, on the ground that the unity of Christian faith between the Abyssinians and the Byzantines prevented him from taking any such action. Saif, disappointed and hopeless, went to Nu'mân ibn al Mundhir, Prince of Hira. This prince presented Saif to Khosroes Noushirwan, King of Persia, to whom he explained the object of his mission. Khosroes at first was unwilling to undertake so dangerous an enterprise, but afterwards, won over by the promises of Saif and the advice of his ministers, sent an army of 4,000 Persian soldiers, drawn from prisons, under the command of Wahriz and accompanied by Saif himself.

The army advanced to Hadramaut, where it was joined by Saif's own adherents, 2,000 strong, and attacked Masrouq, who was defeated and slain in battle. Saif was installed king over Himyar but subject to Khosroes Noushirwan. His first act was to expel from Himyar most of the Abyssinian residents, among whom were many Christians. Subsequently, Saif was murdered by some Abyssinian members of his own court; and after his death no more native Himyarite princes were placed on the throne. He was succeeded first by Wahriz, leader of the Persian army, then by Zin, Binegan, Chore, Chosrau, and Badhan, the last of whom was the governor of Himyar at the time of Mohammed's conquest of Arabia. With the overthrow of the Abyssinian Dynasty in the south, the increase of factional rivalries between the Byzantine and the Persian Empires in the north, and the advent of Islam, Christianity in Arabia came to an end. It must not be imagined, however, that this violent end came without heroic resistance. The famous church, built by Abramos at Sanaa, was still in a flourishing condition at the time of Mohammed, who speaks of his own visit to it, and of listening to the sermons of its famous and eloquent bishop, Quss ibn Sa'ida. The Christians of Najran successfully resisted, during the life of the Prophet, all attempts at Islamic proselytism, although, under 'Omar, Mohammed's second successor (634-644), they were finally compelled to embrace Islam; many refused to do so and were expelled. These migrated to Kufa and Hira, on the Euphrates, where, towards the end of the eighth century, the Nestorian patriarch, Timotheus I (778-820), appointed over them a bishop with both native and Nestorian clergy schools and churches.

Christianity, in the time of Mohammed, under one form or another, must have had also some followers in Hijaz, the stronghold of Islam, and especially around Mecca. Slaves were not infrequently Christian captives brought in by the trading Arabs in their journeys to Syria and Mesopotamia. An Arab poet, quoted by Wellhausen (*Skizzen und Vorarbeiten*, IV, 200), says: "Whence has Al-A'sha his Christian ideas? From the wine-traders of Hira of whom he bought his wine; they brought them to him." These Christian influences are clearly visible in the Koran. Among the early friends and followers of the Prophet were Zaid, his adopted son, who was of Christian parentage, and many others, who, like the three famous hanif (which is translated by many as "hermits", "monks", etc.), abandoned Christianity for Islam. One of these, Warqa, is credited by Moslem writers with a knowledge of the Christian Scriptures, and even with having translated some portions of them into Arabic. Father L. Sheikho, S.J., of the Catholic University of Beirut, Syria, has made a good collection of extracts from ante-Islamic and immediately post-Islamic Arabic poets, in which Christian ideas, beliefs, and practices are alluded to. (See "Al-Mashriq" in "The Orient" of 1905, also published separately.)

At Medina, the Prophet is said to have received repeated embassies from Christian tribes. His treatment of the Christian Arabs was distinctly more liberal and courteous than that accorded by him to the Jews. He looked on the latter as a dangerous political menace, while he regarded the former not only as subjects, but also as friends and allies. In one of his supposed letters to the Bishop Ka'b of the tribe of Harith, to the Bishop of Najran, and to their priests and monks, we read: "There shall be guaranteed to you the protection of God and His Apostles for the possession of your churches and your worship and your monasteries, and no bishop or priest, or monk, shall be molested...so long as you remain true and fulfil your obligations." To Bishop Yuhanna ibn Ruba and to the chiefs of the people of Ayla he wrote: "Peace to you. I commend you to God besides Whom there is no God. I would not war against you without first writing to you. Either accept Islam or pay poll-tax. And hearken to God and His Apostle and to these envoys.... If you turn my envoys back and are not friendly to them then I will accept no reparation from you, but I will war against you and will take the children captive and will slay the aged.... If you will hearken to my envoys, then shall you be under God's protection and Mohammed's and that of his allies." — W. A. Shedd, *Islam and the Oriental Churches* (1904), 103. To the heathen Arabs he held out no compromise; they had either to embrace Islam or die; but to the Christians of his country he always showed himself generous and tolerant, although the Mohammedan tradition tells us that on his deathbed he changed his policy towards them and is said to have commanded that none but Moslems should dwell in the land. In one of his controversies with the Christian tribe of Taghlib, Mohammed agreed that the adults should remain Christian but the children should not be baptized (Wellhausen, op. cit.). The feelings between the Christian and the Mohammedan Arabs were so friendly at the time of the Prophet that many of the latter sought refuge with the former on more than one occasion. Under 'Omar, Mohammed's second successor, however, the policy of Islam towards the Christians completely changed, as can be seen from the so-called "Constitution of 'Omar," which, though generally regarded as spurious, cannot be entirely disregarded.

'Omar's policy practically put an end to Christianity in Arabia, and certainly dealt a death-blow to the Christian religion in the newly conquered West-Asiatic provinces. This extinction and dissolution was violent, but gradual in the peninsula, where many Christians, moved by the wonderful success of the Moslem arms, abandoned their religion and accepted Islam. Some preferred to pay the poll-tax and retain their faith. Others, like the Najranites, in spite of the promise of Mohammed that they should be undisturbed, were forced to leave Arabia and settled partly in Syria and partly near Kufa in lower Mesopotamia (Muir, *History of the Caliphate*, 150; and Arnold, *Preaching of Islam*, 44 sqq.). The tribe of Taghlib was true to its faith, and Bar-Hebræus tells us of two of its chieftains who later suffered martyrdom (*Chronicon Syriacum*, 112, 115). We continue to hear for a long time of Jacobite and Nestorian bishops of the Arabs, one even being Bishop of Sanaa, Yemen, and Bahrein, and of the border regions [Bar-Hebræus, *Chronicon Ecclesiasticum*, I, 303; III, 123, 193; and Thomas of Marga, *Book of Governors* (ed. Budge, 1893), II, 448 sqq.].

Under the Umayyad and Abbasid Caliphs, Christianity enjoyed, with few exceptions, great freedom and respect throughout all the Mohammedan Empire, as can be seen from the facts and data collected by Assemani and Bar-Hebræus, according to which many Nestorian and Jacobite patriarchs from the seventh to the eleventh centuries received diplomas, or firmans, of some sort from Mohammed himself, from Umar, Ali, Merwan, Al-Mansur, Harounal-Raschid, Abu Ja'far, and others. (Shedd, op. cit., 239-241; Assemani, *De Catholicis Nestorianis*, 41-433 sqq.; Bar-Hebraeus, *Chronicon Ecclesiasticum*, I, 309, 317, 319, 325; II, 465, 625; III, 307, 317, 229, 433, etc.; and Thomas of Marga, op. cit., II, 123, note.)

In conclusion, a few words may be said of the various sects and creeds to which the Christian Arabs of the north and of the south belonged, as well as of their practical observance of the Christian religion and duties. We have already seen how that part of Arabia adjacent to the Syrian borders was, from the third century on, regarded as the "mother of heresies". The religious and political freedom of the Arab tribes opened the door to all creeds, errors, and heresies. Before the rise and spread of Nestorianism and Monophysitism, the Arian heresy was the prevailing creed of the Christian Arabs. In the fifth, sixth, and seventh centuries Arianism was supplanted by Nestorianism and Monophysitism, which had then become the official creeds of the two most representative Churches of Syria, Egypt, Abyssinia, Mesopotamia, and Persia. Like the Arabian Jews, the

Christian Arabs did not, as a rule, particularly in the times immediately before and after Mohammed, attach much importance to the practical observance of their religion. The Arabs of pre-Islamic times were notorious for their indifference to their theoretical and practical religious beliefs and observances. Every religion and practice was welcomed so long as it was compatible with Arab freedom of conscience and sensuality; and, as Wellhausen truly remarks, although Christian thought and sentiment could have been infused among the Arabs only through the channel of poetry, it is in this that Christian spirituality performs rather a silent part (op. cit., 203).

Arabian Christianity was a seed sown on stony ground, whose product had no power of resistance when the heat came; it perished without leaving a trace when Islam appeared. It seems strange that these Christian Arabs, who had bishops, and priests, and churches, and even heresies, of their own apparently took no steps towards translating into their language any of the Old and New Testament books; or, if any such translation existed, it has left no trace. The same strange fact is also true in the case of the numerous Jews of Yemen (Margoliouth, op. cit., 35, and Harnack, *Expansion of Christianity*, II, 300). Of these Emmanuel Deutsch remarks that, "Acquainted with the Halachah and Haggada, they seemed, under the peculiar story-loving influence of their countrymen, to have cultivated the latter with all its gorgeous hues and colours" [Remains of Emmanuel Deutsch, *Islam* (New York), 92]. As to the Christians, at least the bishops, the priests, and the monks must have had some religious books; but as we know nothing of their existence, we are forced to suppose that these books were written in a language which they learned abroad, probably in Syria.

BIBLIOGRAPHY. NIEBUHR, *Travels Through Arabia* (tr., Edinburgh, 1792); CAUSSIN DE PERCEVAL, *Essai sur l'histoire des Arabes avant l'Islamisme*, etc. (Paris, 1847); SEDILLOT, *Histoire generale des Arabes* (Paris, 1877); SPRENGER, *Die alte Geographie Arabiens als Grundlage der Entwicklungsgeschichte des Semitismus* (Berne, 1875); PALGRAVE, *Travels in Eastern Arabia* (London, 1893); HAMADANI, *Geography of the Arabian Peninsula* (ed. Mueller, 1891); WELLHAUSEN, *Reste arabischen Heidenthums* (Berlin, 1897); BEKRI AND YAQUT, *Geographical Dictionaries* (ed., Wüstenfield, 1866-70); HOMMEL, *Sudarabische Chrestomathie* (Munich, 1893); GLASER, *Die Abessinier in Arabien und Africa* (Munich, 1895); and *Skizze der Geschichte und Geographie Arabiens* (Berlin, 1890); WINCKLER, *Altorientalische Forschungen* (1st and 2d series, 1893-98); HOGARTH, *Unveiling of Arabia* (London, 1904); BRUENOW, *Die Provincia Arabia* (2 vols. fol., 1905); MARGOLIOUTH in HAST., *Dict. of the Bible*, s.v.; HELEVY in VIG., *Dict. de la Bible*, s.v.

Besides the Fathers and ecclesiastical writers quoted in the body of the article, the reader is referred to the following modern authorities: WRIGHT, *Early Christianity in Arabia*

(London, 1855); WELLHAUSEN, *Juden und Christen in Arabien*, III; *Skizzen und Vorarbeiten*, III, 197 sqq.; NÖLDEKE, *Geschichte der Perser und Araber zur Zeit der Sassaniden aus der arabischen Chronik des Tabari* (Leyden, 1879); CAUSSIN DE PERCEVAL, *Histoire des Arabes avant Mohammet* (Paris, 1847), I, 108, 112, 114, 124-128; II, 47-56, 58, 136, 142, 144, 200-202, 213-215; III, 275; DUCHESNE, *Les églises séparées* (2d ed., Paris, 1905) 300-352; ZWEMER, *Arabia: The Cradle of Islam* (New York, 1900), 300-313; SHEDD, *Islam and the Oriental Churches* (Philadelphia, 1904); HARNACK, *The Expansion of Christianity in the First Three Centuries* (tr. London, 1905), 300-304; MARGOLIOUTH, *Mohammed and the Rise of Islam* (London, 1905), 33 sqq. Among Syriac writers see: BAR-HEBRÆUS, *Chronicum Ecclesiasticum*, ed. ABBELOOS and LAMY (Louvain, 1874), II; MARIS, *Amri et Slibœ Liber Turris*, ed. GISMONDI, (Rome, 1896, 1899); ASSEMANI, *Bibliotheca Orientalis*, III, pt. 2, 591-610, and passim; LEQUIEN, *Oriens Christianus*, II; CHABOT, *Synodicon Orientale* (Paris, 1902), passim; LABOURT, *Le Christianisme dans l'empire perse sous la dynastie sassanide* (Paris, 1904). See also BARONIUS, PAGI, and TILLEMONT. On the massacre of the Christians of Najran, see the letter of SIMEON, Bishop of Beth-Arsam, the best edition of which is given by GUIDI in the *Memorie dell' accademia dei Lincei* (Rome, 1880-81, in Syriac and in Italian). The Greek hymn of JOHN THE PSALMIST is translated into Syriac by PAUL, Bishop of Edessa (d. 526), and edited by SCHRÖTER in the *Zeitschrift für deutsche morgenlaendische Gesellschaft*, XXXI, together with the letter of JAMES OF SARUG. See also BOISSONADE, *Anecdota Græca*, V, 1, *Martyrium Arethae*, and *Acta SS.*, X, 721. The supposed theological dispute between Gregentius and Herban is found in BOISSONADE, *Anecdota Græca*, V, 63; and *P.G.*, LXXVI, 568.

GABRIEL OUSSANI

The Great and Enduring Heresy of Mohammed

Hilaire Belloc

It might have appeared to any man watching affairs in the earlier years of the seventh century — say from 600 to 630—that only one great main assault having been made against the Church, Arianism and its derivatives, that assault having been repelled and the Faith having won its victory, it was now secure for an indefinite time.

Christendom would have to fight for its life, of course, against outward unchristian things, that is, against Paganism. The nature worshippers of the high Persian civilization to the east would attack us in arms and try to overwhelm us. The savage paganism of barbaric tribes, Scandinavian, German, Slav and Mongol, in the north and centre of Europe would also attack Christendom and try to destroy it. The populations subject to Byzantium would continue to parade heretical views as a label for their grievances. But the main effort of heresy, at least, had failed — so it seemed. Its object, the undoing of a united Catholic civilization, had been missed. The rise of no major heresy need henceforth be feared, still less the consequent disruption of Christendom.

By A.D. 630 all Gaul had long been Catholic. The last of the Arian generals and their garrisons in Italy and Spain had become orthodox. The Arian generals and garrisons of Northern Africa had been conquered by the orthodox armies of the Emperor.

It was just at this moment, a moment of apparently universal and permanent Catholicism, that there fell an unexpected blow of overwhelming magnitude and force. Islam arose — quite suddenly. It came out of the desert and overwhelmed half our civilization.

Islam — the teaching of Mohammed — conquered immediately in arms. Mohammed's Arabian converts charged into Syria and won there two great battles, the first upon the Yarmuk to the east of Palestine in the highlands above the Jordan, the second in Mesopotamia. They went on to overrun Egypt; they pushed further and further into the heart of our Christian civilization with all its grandeur of Rome. They established themselves all over Northern Africa; they raided into Asia Minor, though they did not establish themselves there as yet. They could even occasionally threaten Constantinople itself. At last, a long lifetime after their first victories in Syria, they crossed the Straits of Gibraltar into Western Europe and began to flood Spain. They even got as far as the very heart of Northern France between Poitiers and Tours, less than a hundred years after their first victories in Syria — in A.D. 732. They were ultimately thrust back to the Pyrenees, but they continued to hold all Spain except the mountainous north-western corner. They held all Roman Africa, including Egypt, and all Syria. They dominated the whole Mediterranean west and east: held its islands, raided and left armed settlements even on the shores of Gaul and Italy. They spread mightily throughout Hither Asia, overwhelming the Persian realm. They were an increasing menace to Constantinople. Within a hundred years, a main part of the Roman world had fallen under the power of this new and strange force from the Desert.

Such a revolution had never been. No earlier attack had been so sudden, so violent or so permanently successful. Within a score of years from the first assault in 634 the Christian Levant had gone; Syria, the cradle of the Faith, and Egypt with Alexandria, the mighty Christian See. Within a lifetime half the wealth and nearly half the territory of the Christian Roman Empire was in the hands of Mohammedan masters and officials, and the mass of the population was becoming affected more and more by this new thing.

Mohammedan government and influence had taken the place of Christian government and influence, and were on the way to making the bulk of the Mediterranean on the east and the south Mohammedan.

We are about to follow the fortunes of this extraordinary thing which still calls itself Islam, that is, "The Acceptation" of the morals and simple doctrines which Mohammed had preached.

I shall later describe the historical origin of the thing, giving the dates of its progress and the stages of its original success. I shall describe the consolidation of it, its increasing power and the threat which it remained to our civilization. It very nearly destroyed us. It kept up the battle against Christendom actively for a thousand years, and the story is by no means over; the power of Islam may at any moment re-arise.

But before following that story we must grasp the two fundamental things — *first*, the nature of Mohammedanism; *second*, the essential cause of its sudden and, as it were, miraculous success over so many thousands of miles of territory and so many millions of human beings.

Mohammedanism was a *heresy*: that is the essential point to grasp before going any further. It began as a heresy, not as a new religion. It was not a pagan contrast with the Church; it was not an alien enemy. It was a perversion of Christian doctrine. Its vitality and endurance soon gave it the appearance of a new religion, but those who were contemporary with its rise saw it for what it was — not a denial, but an adaptation and a misuse, of the Christian thing. It differed from most (not from all) heresies in this, that it did not arise within the bounds of the Christian Church. The chief heresiarch, Mohammed himself, was not, like most heresiarchs, a man of Catholic birth and doctrine to begin with. He sprang from pagans. But that which he taught was in the main Catholic doctrine, oversimplified. It was the great Catholic world — on the frontiers of which he lived, whose influence was all around him and whose territories he had known by travel — which inspired his convictions. He came of, and mixed with, the degraded idolaters of the Arabian wilderness, the conquest of which had never seemed worth the Romans' while.

He took over very few of those old pagan ideas which might have been native to him from his descent. On the contrary, he preached and insisted upon a whole group of ideas which were peculiar to the Catholic Church and distinguished it from the paganism which it had conquered in the Greek and Roman civilization. Thus the very foundation of his teaching was that prime Catholic doctrine, the unity and omnipotence of God. The attributes of God he also took over in the main from Catholic doctrine: the personal nature, the all-goodness, the timelessness, the providence of God, His creative power as the origin of all things, and His sustenance of all things by His power alone. The world of good spirits and angels and of evil spirits in rebellion against God was part of the teaching, with a chief evil spirit, such as Christendom had recognized. Mohammed preached with insistence that prime Catholic doctrine, on the human side — the immortality of the soul and its responsibility for actions in this life, coupled with the consequent doctrine of punishment and reward after death.

If anyone sets down those points that orthodox Catholicism has in common with Mohammedanism, and those points only, one might imagine if one went no further that there should have been no cause of quarrel. Mohammed would almost seem in this aspect to be a sort of missionary, preaching and spreading by the energy of his character the chief and fundamental doctrines of the Catholic Church among those who had hitherto been degraded pagans of the Desert. He gave to Our Lord the highest reverence, and to Our

Lady also, for that matter. On the day of judgment (another Catholic idea which he taught) it was Our Lord, according to Mohammed, who would be the judge of mankind, not he, Mohammed. The Mother of Christ, Our Lady, "the Lady Miriam" was ever for him the first of womankind. His followers even got from the early fathers some vague hint of her Immaculate Conception.[1]

But the central point where this new heresy struck home with a mortal blow against Catholic tradition was a full denial of the Incarnation.

Mohammed did not merely take the first steps toward that denial, as the Arians and their followers had done; he advanced a clear affirmation, full and complete, against the whole doctrine of an incarnate God. He taught that Our Lord was the greatest of all the prophets, but still only a prophet: a man like other men. He eliminated the Trinity altogether.

With that denial of the Incarnation went the whole sacramental structure. He refused to know anything of the Eucharist, with its Real Presence; he stopped the sacrifice of Mass, and therefore the institution of a

[1] It was from this fact that certain French writers opposed to the Church got their enormous blunder, that the Immaculate Conception came to us from Mohammedan sources! Gibbon, of course, copied his masters blindly here—as he always does, and he repeats the absurdity in his " Decline and Fall."

107

special priesthood. In other words, he, like so many other lesser heresiarchs, founded his heresy on simplification.

Catholic doctrine was true (he seemed to say), but it had become encumbered with false accretions; it had become complicated by needless man-made additions, including the idea that its founder was Divine, and the growth of a parasitical caste of priests who battened on a late, imagined, system of Sacraments which they alone could administer. All those corrupt accretions must be swept away.

There is thus a very great deal in common between the enthusiasm with which Mohammed's teaching attacked the priesthood, the Mass and the sacraments, and the enthusiasm with which Calvinism, the central motive force of the Reformation, did the same. As we all know, the new teaching relaxed the marriage laws — but in practice this did not affect the mass of his followers who still remained monogamous. It made divorce as easy as possible, for the sacramental idea of marriage disappeared. It insisted upon the equality of men, and it necessarily had that further factor in which it resembled Calvinism — the sense of predestination, the sense of fate; of what the followers of John Knox were always calling "the immutable decrees of God."

Mohammed's teaching never developed among the mass of his followers, or in his own mind, a detailed theology. He was content to accept all that appealed to him in the Catholic scheme and to reject all that seemed to him, and to so many others of his time, too complicated or mysterious to be true. Simplicity was the note of the whole affair; and since all heresies draw their strength from some true doctrine, Mohammedanism drew its strength from the true Catholic doctrines which it retained; the equality of men before God — "All true believers are brothers." It zealously preached and throve on the paramount claims of justice, social and economic.

Now, why did this new, simple, energetic heresy have its sudden overwhelming success?

One answer is that it won battles. It won them at once, and thoroughly, as we shall see when we come to the history of the thing. But winning battles would not have made Islam permanent or even strong had there not been a state of affairs awaiting some such message and ready to accept it.

Both in the world of Hither Asia and in the Græco-Roman world of the Mediterranean, but especially in the latter, society had fallen, much as our society has today, into a tangle wherein the bulk of men were disappointed and angry and seeking for a solution to the whole group of social strains. There was indebtedness everywhere; the power of money and consequent usury. There was slavery everywhere.

Society reposed upon it, as ours resposes upon wage slavery today. There was weariness and discontent with theological debate, which, for all its intensity, had grown out of touch with the masses. There lay upon the freemen, already tortured with debt, a heavy burden of imperial taxation; and there was the irritant of existing central government interfering with men's lives; there was the tyranny of the lawyers and their charges.

To all this Islam came as a vast relief and a solution of strain. The slave who admitted that Mohammed was the prophet of God and that the new teaching had, therefore, divine authority, ceased to be a slave. The slave who adopted Islam was henceforward free. The debtor who "accepted" was rid of his debts. Usury was forbidden. The small farmer was relieved not only of his debts but of his crushing taxation. Above all, justice could be had without buying it from lawyers.... All this in theory. The practice was not nearly so complete. Many a convert remained a debtor, many were still slaves. But wherever Islam conquered there was a new spirit of freedom and relaxation.

It was the combination of all these things, the attractive simplicity of the doctrine, the sweeping away of clerical and imperial discipline, the huge immediate practical advantage of freedom for the slave and riddance of anxiety for the debtor, the crowning advantage of free justice under few and simple new laws easily understood—that formed the driving force behind the astonishing Mohammedan social victory. The courts were everywhere accessible to all without payment and giving verdicts which all could understand. The Mohammedan movement was essentially a "Reformation," and we can discover numerous affinities between Islam and the Protestant Reformers — on Images, on the Mass, on Celibacy, etc.

The marvel seems to be, not so much that the new emancipation swept over men much as we might imagine Communism to sweep over our industrial world today, but that there should still have remained, as there remained for generations, a prolonged and stubborn resistance to Mohammedanism.

There you have, I think, the nature of Islam and of its first original blaze of victory.

We have just seen what was the main cause of Islam's extraordinarily rapid spread; a complicated and fatigued society, and one burdened with the institution of slavery; one, moreover, in which millions of peasants in Egypt, Syria and all the East, crushed with usury and heavy taxation, were offered immediate relief by the new creed, or rather, the new heresy. Its note was simplicity and therefore it was suited to the popular mind in a society where hitherto a restricted class had pursued its quarrels on theology and government.

That is the main fact which accounts for the sudden spread of Islam after its first armed victory over the armies rather than the people of the Greek-speaking Eastern empire. But this alone would not account for two other equally striking triumphs. The first was the power the new heresy showed of absorbing the Asiatic people of the Near East, Mesopotamia and the mountain land between it and India. The second was the wealth and splendour of the Caliphate (that is, of the central Mohammedan monarchy) in the generations coming immediately after the first sweep of victory.

The first of these points, the spread over Mesopotamia and Persia and the mountain land towards India, was not, as in the case of the sudden successes in Syria and Egypt, due to the appeal of simplicity, freedom from slavery and relief from debt. It was due to a certain underlying historical character in the Near East which has always influenced its society and continues to influence it today. That character is a sort of natural uniformity. There has been inherent in it from times earlier than any known historical record, a sort of instinct for obedience to one religious head, which is also the civil head, and a general similarity of social culture. When we talk of the age-long struggle between Asia and the West, we mean by the word "Asia" all that sparse population of the mountain land beyond Mesopotamia towards India, its permanent influence upon the Mesopotamian plains themselves, and its potential influence upon even the highlands and sea coast of Syria and Palestine.

The struggle between Asia and Europe swings over a vast period like a tide ebbing and flowing. For nearly a thousand years, from the conquest of Alexander to the coming of the Mohammedan Reformers (333 B.C.-A.D. 634), the tide had set eastward; that is, western influences — Greek, and then Greek and Roman—had flooded the debatable land. For a short period of about two and a half to three centuries even Mesopotamia was superficially Greek — in its governing class, at any rate. Then Asia began to flood back again westward. The old Pagan Roman Empire and the Christian Empire, which succeeded it and which was governed from Constantinople, were never able to hold permanently the land beyond the Euphrates. The new push from Asia westward was led by the Persians, and the Persians and Parthians (which last were a division of the Persians) not only kept their hold on Mesopotamia but were able to carry out raids into Roman territory itself, right up to the end of that period. In the last few years before the appearance of Mohammedanism they had appeared on the

Mediterranean coast and had sacked Jerusalem.

Now when Islam came with its first furious
victorious cavalry charges springing from the desert, it
powerfully reinforced this tendency of Asia to reassert
itself. The uniformity of temper which is the mark of
Asiatic society, responded at once to this new idea of
one very simple, personal form of government,
sanctified by religion, and ruling with a power
theoretically absolute from one centre. The Caliphate
once established at Baghdad, Baghdad became just
what Babylon had been; the central capital of one vast
society, giving its tone to all the lands from the Indian
borders to Egypt and beyond.

But even more remarkable than the flooding of all
near Asia with Mohammedanism in one lifetime was
the wealth and splendour and culture of the new
Islamic Empire. Islam was in those early centuries
(most of the seventh, all the eighth and ninth), the
highest material civilization of our occidental world.
The city of Constantinople was also very wealthy and
enjoyed a very high civilization, which radiated over
dependent provinces, Greece and the seaboard of the
Ægean and the uplands of Asia Minor, but it was
focussed in the imperial city; in the greater part of the
countrysides culture was on the decline. In the West it
was notoriously so. Gaul and Britain, and in some

degree Italy, and the valley of the Danube, fell back towards barbarism. They never became completely barbaric, not even Britain, which was the most remote; but they were harried and impoverished, and lacked proper government. From the fifth century to the early eleventh (say A.D. 450 to A.D. 1030) ran the period which we call "The Dark Ages" of Europe — in spite of Charlemagne's experiment.

So much for the Christian world of that time, against which Islam was beginning to press so heavily; which had lost to Islam the whole of Spain and certain islands and coasts of the central Mediterranean as well. Christendom was under siege from Islam. Islam stood up against us in dominating splendour and wealth and power, and, what was even more important, with superior knowledge in the practical and applied sciences.

Islam preserved the Greek philosophers, the Greek mathematicians and their works, the physical science of the Greek and Roman earlier writers. Islam was also far more lettered than was Christendom. In the mass of the West most men had become illiterate. Even in Constantinople reading and writing were not as common as they were in the world governed by the Caliph.

One might sum up and say that the contrast

between the Mohammedan world of those early centuries and the Christian world which it threatened to overwhelm was like the contrast between a modern industrialized state and a backward, half-developed state next door to it: the contrast between modern Germany, for instance, and its Russian neighbour. The contrast was not as great as that, but the modern parallel helps one to understand it. For centuries to come Islam was to remain a menace, even though Spain was re-conquered. In the East it became more than a menace, and spread continually for seven hundred years, until it had mastered the Balkans and the Hungarian plain, and all but occupied Western Europe itself. Islam was the one heresy that nearly destroyed Christendom through its early material and intellectual superiority.

Now why was this? It seems inexplicable when we remember the uncertain and petty personal leaderships, the continual changes of local dynasties, the shifting foundation of the Mohammedan effort. That effort began with the attack of a very few thousand desert horsemen, who were as much drawn by desire for loot as by their enthusiasm for their new doctrines. Those doctrines had been preached to a very sparse body of nomads, boasting but very few permanently inhabited centres. They had originated in a man remarkable indeed for the intensity of his nature, probably more than half convinced, probably also a little mad, and one who had never shown constructive ability — yet Islam conquered.

Mohammed was a camel driver, who had had the good luck to make a wealthy marriage with a woman older than himself. From the security of that position he worked out his visions and enthusiasms, and undertook his propaganda. But it was all done in an ignorant and very small way. There was no organization, and the moment the first bands had succeeded in battle, the leaders began fighting among themselves: not only fighting, but murdering. The story of all the first lifetime, and a little more, after the original rush — the story of the Mohammedan government (such as it was) so long as it was centred in Damascus, is a story of successive intrigue and murder. Yet when the second dynasty which presided for so long over Islam, the Abbasides, with their capital further east at Baghdad, on the Euphrates, restored the old Mesopotamian domination over Syria, ruling also Egypt and all the Mohammedan world, that splendour and science, material power and wealth of which I spoke, arose and dazzled all contemporaries, and we must ask the question again: why was this?

The answer lies in the very nature of the Mohammedan conquest. It did *not*, as has been so frequently repeated, destroy at once what it came across;

it did *not* exterminate all those who would not accept Islam. It was just the other way. It was remarkable among all the powers which have ruled these lands throughout history for what has wrongly been called its "tolerance." The Mohammedan temper was not tolerant. It was, on the contrary, fanatical and bloodthirsty. It felt no respect for, nor even curiosity about, those from whom it differed. It was absurdly vain of itself, regarding with contempt the high Christian culture about it. It still so regards it even today.

But the conquerors, and those whom they converted and attached to themselves from the native populations, were still too few to govern by force. And (what is more important) they had no idea of organization. They were always slipshod and haphazard. Therefore a very large majority of the conquered remained in their old habits of life and of religion.

Slowly the influence of Islam spread through these, but during the first centuries the great majority in Syria, and even in Mesopotamia and Egypt, were Christian, keeping the Christian Mass, the Christian Gospels, and all the Christian tradition. It was they who preserved the Græco-Roman civilization from which they descended, and it was that civilization, surviving under the surface of Mohammedan government, which gave their learning and material power to the wide territories which we must call, even so early, "the Mohammedan world," though the bulk of it was not yet Mohammedan in creed.

But there was another and it is the most important cause. The fiscal cause: the overwhelming wealth of the early Mohammedan Caliphate. The merchant and the tiller of the land, the owner of property and the negotiator, were everywhere relieved by the Mohammedan conquest; for a mass of usury was swept away, as was an intricate system of taxation which had become clogged, ruining the taxpayer without corresponding results for the government. What the Arabian conquerors and their successors in Mesopotamia did was to replace all that by a simple, straight system of tribute.

Whatever was not Mohammedan in the immense Mohammedan Empire — that is, much the most of its population — was subject to a special tribute; and it was this tribute which furnished directly, without loss from the intricacies of bureaucracy, the wealth of the central power: the revenue of the Caliph. That revenue remained enormous during all the first generations. The result was that which always follows upon a high concentration of wealth in one governing centre; the whole of the society governed from that centre reflects the opulence of its directors.

There we have the explanation of that strange, that

unique phenomenon in history — a revolt against civilization which did not destroy civilization; a consuming heresy which did not destroy the Christian religion against which it was directed.

The world of Islam became, and long remained, the heir of the old Graeco-Roman culture and the preserver thereof. Thence was it that, alone of all the great heresies, Mohammedanism not only survived, and is, after nearly fourteen centuries, as strong as ever spiritually. In time it struck roots and established a civilization of its own over against ours, and a permanent rival to us.

Now that we have understood why Islam, the most formidable of the heresies, achieved its strength and astounding success we must try to understand why, alone of all the heresies, it has survived in full strength and even continues (after a fashion) to expand to this day.

This is a point of decisive importance to the understanding not only of our subject but of the history of the world in general. Yet it is one which is, unfortunately, left almost entirely undiscussed in the modern world.

Millions of modern people of the white civilization — that is, the civilization of Europe and America — have forgotten all about Islam. They have never come in contact with it. They take for granted that it is decaying, and that, anyway, it is just a foreign religion which will not concern them. It is, as a fact, the most formidable and persistent enemy which our civilization has had, and may at any moment become as large a menace in the future as it has been in the past.

To that point of its future menace I shall return in the last of these pages on Mohammedanism.

All the great heresies — save this one of Mohammedanism — seem to go through the same phases.

First they rise with great violence and become fashionable; they do so by insisting on some one of the great Catholic doctrines in an exaggerated fashion; and because the great Catholic doctrines combined form the only full and satisfactory philosophy known to mankind, each doctrine is bound to have its special appeal.

Thus Arianism insisted on the unity of God, combined with the majesty and creative power of Our Lord. At the same time it appealed to imperfect minds because it tried to rationalize a mystery. Calvinism again had a great success because it insisted on another main doctrine, the Omnipotence and Omniscience of God. It got the rest out of proportion and went violently wrong on Predestination; but it had its moment of triumph when it looked as though it were going to conquer all our civilization—which it would have done if the French had not fought it in their great religious war and conquered its adherents on that soil of Gaul which has always been the battle ground and testing place of European ideas.

After this first phase of the great heresies, when they are in their initial vigour and spread like a flame from man to man, there comes a second phase of decline, lasting, apparently (according to some obscure law), through about five or six generations: say a couple of hundred years or a little more. The adherents of the heresy grow less numerous and less convinced until at last only quite a small number can be called full and faithful followers of the original movement.

Then comes the third phase, when each heresy wholly disappears as a bit of doctrine: no one believes the doctrine any more or only such a tiny fraction remain believers that they no longer count. But the social and moral factors of the heresy remain and may be of powerful effect for generations more. We see that in the case of Calvinism today. Calvinism produced the Puritan movement and from that there proceeded as a necessary consequence the isolation of the soul, the break up of corporate social action, unbridled competition and greed, and at last the full establishment of what we call "Industrial Capitalism" today, whereby civilization is now imperilled through the discontent of the vast destitute majority with their few plutocratic masters. There is no one left except perhaps a handful of people in Scotland who really believe the doctrines Calvin taught, but the spirit of Calvinism is still very strong in the countries it originally infected, and its social fruits remain.

Now in the case of Islam none of all this happened except the *first* phase. There was no second phase of gradual decline in the numbers and conviction of its followers. On the contrary Islam grew from strength to strength acquiring more and more territory, converting more and more followers, until it had established itself as a quite separate civilization and seemed so like a new religion that most people came to forget its origin as a heresy.

Islam increased not only in numbers and in the conviction of its followers but in territory and in actual political and armed power until close on the eighteenth century. Less than 100 years before the American War of Independence a Mohammedan army was threatening to overrun and destroy Christian civilization, and would have done so if the Catholic King of Poland had not destroyed that army outside Vienna.

Since then the armed power of Mohammedanism has declined, but neither its numbers nor the conviction of its followers have appreciably declined;

and as to the territory annexed by it, though it has lost places in which it ruled over subject Christian majorities, it has gained new adherents — to some extent in Asia, and largely in Africa. Indeed in Africa it is still expanding among the negroid populations, and that expansion provides an important future problem for the European Governments who have divided Africa between them.

And there is another point in connection with this power of Islam. Islam is apparently *unconvertible*.

The missionary efforts made by great Catholic orders which have been occupied in trying to turn Mohammedans into Christians for nearly 400 years have everywhere wholly failed. We have in some places driven the Mohammedan master out and freed his Christian subjects from Mohammedan control, but we have had hardly any effect in converting individual Mohammedans save perhaps to some small amount in Southern Spain 500 years ago; and even so that was rather an example of political than of religious change.

Now what is the explanation of all this? Why should Islam alone of all the great heresies show such continued vitality?

Those who are sympathetic with Mohammedanism and still more those who are actually Mohammedans explain it by proclaiming it the best and most human

124

of religions, the best suited to mankind, and the most attractive.

Strange as it may seem, there are a certain number of highly educated men, European gentlemen, who have actually joined Islam, that is, who are personal converts to Mohammedanism. I myself have known and talked to some half-dozen of them in various parts of the world, and there are a very much larger number of similar men, well instructed Europeans, who, having lost their faith in Catholicism or in some form of Protestantism in which they were brought up, feel sympathy with the Mohammedan social scheme although they do not actually join it or profess belief in its religion. We constantly meet men of this kind today among those who have travelled in the East.

These men always give the same answer — Islam is indestructible because it is founded on simplicity and justice. It has kept those Christian doctrines which are evidently true and which appeal to the common sense of millions, while getting rid of priestcraft, mysteries, sacraments, and all the rest of it. It proclaims and practises human equality. It loves justice and forbids usury. It produces a society in which men are happier and feel their own dignity more than in any other. That is its strength and that is why it still converts people and endures and will perhaps return to power in the near future.

Now I do not think that explanation to be the true one. All heresy talks in those terms. Every heresy will tell you that it has purified the corruptions of Christian doctrines and in general done nothing but good to mankind, satisfied the human soul, and so on. Yet every one of them *except* Mohammedanism has faded out. Why?

In order to get the answer to the problem we must remark in what the fortunes of Islam have differed from those of all the other great heresies, and when we remark that I think we shall have the clue to the truth.

Islam has differed from all the other heresies in two main points which must be carefully noticed:

(1) It did not rise within the Church, that is, within the frontiers of our civilization. Its heresiarch was not a man originally Catholic who led away Catholic followers by his novel doctrine as did Arius or Calvin. He was an outsider, born a pagan, living among pagans, and never baptized. He adopted Christian doctrines and selected among them in the true heresiarch fashion. He dropped those that did not suit him and insisted on those that did — which is the mark of the heresiarch — but he did not do this as from within; his action was external.

Those first small but fierce armies of nomad Arabs who won their astounding victories in Syria and Egypt against the Catholic world of the early seventh century were made of men who had all been pagans before they became Mohammedan. There was among them no previous Catholicism to which they might return.

(2) This body of Islam attacking Christendom from beyond its frontiers and not breaking it up from within, happened to be continually recruited with fighting material of the strongest kind and drafted in from the pagan outer darkness.

This recruitment went on in waves, incessantly, through the centuries until the end of the Middle Ages. It was mainly Mongol coming from Asia (though some of it was Berber coming from North Africa), and it was this ceaseless, recurrent impact of new adherents, conquerors and fighters as the original Arabs had been, which gave Islam its formidable resistance and continuance of power.

Not long after the first conquest of Syria and Egypt it looked as though the enthusiastic new heresy, in spite of its dazzling sudden triumph, would fail. The continuity in leadership broke down. So did the political unity of the whole scheme. The original capital of the movement was Damascus and at first Mohammedanism was a Syrian thing (and, by extension, an Egyptian thing); but after quite a short time a break-up was apparent. A new dynasty began ruling from Mesopotamia and no longer from Syria. The Western Districts, that is North Africa and Spain (after the conquest of Spain), formed a separate political government under a separate obedience. *But the caliphs at Baghdad began to support themselves by a bodyguard of hired fighters who were Mongols from the steppes of Asia.*

The characteristic of these nomadic Mongols (who come after the fifth century over and over again in waves to the assault against our civilization), is that they are indomitable fighters and at the same time almost purely destructive. They massacre by the million; they burn and destroy; they turn fertile districts into desert. They seem incapable of creative effort.

Twice we in the Christian European West have barely escaped final destruction at their hands; once when we defeated the vast Asiatic army of Attila near Chalons in France, in the middle of the fifth century (not before he had committed horrible outrage and left ruin behind him everywhere), and again in the thirteenth century, 800 years later. Then the advancing Asiatic Mongol power was checked, not by our armies but by the death of the man who had united it in his one hand. But it was not checked till it reached north Italy and was approaching Venice.

It was this recruitment of Mongol bodyguards in

successive instalments which kept Islam going and prevented its suffering the fate that all other heresies had suffered. It kept Islam thundering like a battering ram from *outside the frontiers* of Europe, making breaches in our defence and penetrating further and further into what had been Christian lands.

The Mongol invaders readily accepted Islam; the men who served as mercenary soldiers and formed the real power of the Caliphs were quite ready to conform to the simple requirements of Mohammedanism. They had no regular religion of their own strong enough to counteract the effects of those doctrines of Islam which, mutilated as they were, were in the main Christian doctrines — the unity and majesty of God, the immortality of the soul and all the rest of it. The Mongol mercenaries supporting the political power of the Caliphs were attracted to these main doctrines and easily adopted them. They became good Moslems and as soldiers supporting the Caliphs were thus propagators and maintainers of Islam.

When in the heart of the Middle Ages it looked as though again Islam had failed, a new batch of Mongol soldiers, "Turks" by name, came in and saved the fortunes of Mohammedanism again, although they began by the most abominable destruction of such civilization as Mohammedanism had preserved. That is why in the struggles of the Crusades Christians regarded the enemy as "The Turk"; a general name common to many of these nomad tribes. The Christian preachers of the Crusades and captains of the soldiers and the Crusaders in their songs speak of "The Turk" as the enemy, much more than they do in general of Mohammedanism.

In spite of the advantage of being fed by continual recruitment, the pressure of Mohammedanism upon Christendom might have failed after all, had one supreme attempt to relieve that pressure upon the Christian West succeeded. That supreme attempt was made in the middle of the whole business (A.D. 1095-1200) and is called in history "The Crusades." Catholic Christendom succeeded in recapturing Spain; it nearly succeeded in pushing back Mohammedanism from Syria, in saving the Christian civilization of Asia, and in cutting off the Asiatic Mohammedan from the African. Had it done so perhaps Mohammedanism would have died.

But the Crusades failed. Their failure is the major tragedy in the history of our struggle against Islam, that is, against Asia — against the East.

What the Crusades were, and why and how they failed I shall now describe.

The success of Mohammedanism had not been due

to its offering something more satisfactory in the way of philosophy and morals, but, as I have said, to the opportunity it afforded of freedom to the slave and debtor, and an extreme simplicity which pleased the unintelligent masses who were perplexed by the mysteries inseparable from the profound intellectual life of Catholicism, and from its radical doctrine of the Incarnation. But it was spreading and it looked as though it were bound to win universally, as do all great heresies in their beginnings, because it was the fashionable thing of the time — the conquering thing.

Now against the great heresies, when they acquire the driving power of being the new and fashionable thing, there arises a reaction within the Christian and Catholic mind, which reaction gradually turns the current backward, gets rid of the poison and re-establishes Christian civilization. Such reactions begin, I repeat, obscurely. It is the plain man who gets uncomfortable and says to himself, "This may be the fashion of the moment, but I don't like it." It is the mass of Christian men who feel in their bones that there is something wrong, though they have difficulty in explaining it. The reaction is usually slow and muddled and for a long time not successful. But in the long run with internal heresy it has always succeeded; just as the native health of the human body succeeds in getting rid of some internal infection.

A heresy, when it is full of its original power, affects even Catholic thought — thus Arianism produced a mass of semi-Arianism running throughout Christendom. The Manichean dread of the body and the false doctrine that matter is evil affected even the greatest Catholics of the time. There is a touch of it in the letters of the great St. Gregory. In the same way Mohammedanism had its effect on the Christian Emperors of Byzantium and on Charlemagne, the Emperor of the West; for instance there was a powerful movement started against the use of images, which are so essential to Catholic worship. Even in the West, where Mohammedanism had never reached, the attempt to get rid of images in the churches nearly succeeded.

But while Mohammedanism was spreading, absorbing greater and greater numbers into its own body out of the subject Christian populations of East and North Africa, occupying more and more territory, a defensive reaction against it had begun. Islam gradually absorbed North Africa and crossed over into Spain; less than a century after those first victories in Syria it even pushed across the Pyrenees, right into France. Luckily it was defeated in battle halfway between Tours and Poitiers in the north centre of the country. Some think that if the Christian leaders had not won that battle, the whole of Christendom would have been swamped by Mohammedanism. At any rate from that moment in the West it never advanced further. It was pushed back to the Pyrenees, and very slowly indeed over a period of 300 years it was thrust further and further south towards the centre of Spain, the north of which was cleared again of Mohammedan influence. In the East, however, as we shall see, it continued to be an overwhelming threat.

Now the success of Christian men in pushing back the Mohammedan from France and halfway down Spain began a sort of re-awakening in Europe. It was high time. We of the West had been besieged in three ways; pagan Asiatics had come upon us in the very heart of the Germanics; pagan pirates of the most cruel and disgusting sort had swarmed over the Northern Seas and nearly wiped out Christian civilization in England and hurt it also in Northern France; and with all that there had been this pressure of Moham-medanism coming from the South and South-east — a much more civilized pressure than that of the Asiatics or Scandinavian pirates but still a menace, under which our Christian civilization came near to disappearing.

It is most interesting to take a map of Europe and mark off the extreme limits reached by the enemies of Christendom during the worst of this struggle for existence. The outriders of the worst Asiatic raid got as far as Tournus on the Saône, which is in the very middle of what is France today; the Mohammedan got, as we have seen, to the very middle of France also, somewhere between Tournus and Poitiers. The horrible Scandinavian pagan pirates raided Ireland, all England, and came up all the rivers of Northern France and Northern Germany. They got as far as Cologne, they besieged Paris, they nearly took Hamburg. People today forget how very doubtful a thing it was in the height of the Dark Ages, between the middle of the eighth and the end of the ninth century, whether Catholic civilization would survive at all. Half the Mediterranean Islands had fallen to the Mohammedan, all the Near East; he was fighting to get hold of Asia Minor; and the north and centre of Europe were perpetually raided by the Asiatics and the Northern pagans.

Then came the great reaction and the awakening of Europe.

The chivalry which poured out of Gaul into Spain and the native Spanish knights forcing back the Mohammedans began the affair. The Scandinavian pirates and the raiders from Asia had been defeated two generations before. Pilgrimages to Jerusalem, distant, expensive and perilous, but continuous throughout the Dark Ages, were now especially imperilled through a new Mongol wave of Mohammedan soldiers establishing themselves over the East and especially in Palestine; and the cry arose that the Holy Places, the True Cross (which was preserved in Jerusalem) and the remaining Christian communities of Syria and Palestine, and above all the Holy Sepulchre — the site of the Resurrection, the main object of every pilgrimage — ought to be saved from the usurping hands of Islam. Enthusiastic men preached the duty of marching eastward and rescuing the Holy Land; the reigning Pope, Urban, put himself at the head of the movement in a famous sermon delivered in France to vast crowds, who cried out: "God wills it." Irregular bodies began to pour out eastward for the thrusting back of Islam from the Holy Land, and in due time the regular levies of great Christian Princes prepared for an organized effort on a vast scale. Those who vowed themselves to pursue the effort took the badge of the Cross on their clothing, and from this the struggle became to be known as the Crusades.

The First Crusade was launched in three great bodies of more or less organized Christian soldiery, who set out to march from Western Europe to the Holy Land. I say "more or less organized" because the feudal army was never highly organized; it was divided into units of very different sizes, each following a feudal lord — but of course it had sufficient organization to carry a military enterprise through, because a mere herd of men can never do that. In order not to exhaust the provisions of the countries through which they had to march, the Christian leaders went in three bodies, one from Northern France, going down the valley of the Danube; another from Southern France, going across Italy; and a third of Frenchmen who had recently acquired dominion in Southern Italy and who crossed the Adriatic directly, making for Constantinople through the Balkans. They all joined at Constantinople, and by the time they got there, there were still in spite of losses on the way something which may have been a quarter of a million men — perhaps more. The numbers were never accurately known or computed.

The Emperor at Constantinople was still free, at the head of his great Christian capital, but he was dangerously menaced by the fighting Mohammedan Turks who were only Just over the water in Asia Minor, and whose object it was to get hold of Constantinople and so press on to the ruin of Christendom. This pressure on Constantinople the great mass of the Crusaders immediately relieved; they won a battle against the Turks at Dorylæum and pressed on with great difficulty and further large losses of men till they reached the corner where Syria joins on to Asia Minor at the Gulf of Alexandretta. There, one of the Crusading leaders carved out a kingdom for himself, making his capital at the Christian town of Edessa, to serve as a bulwark against further Mohammedan pressure from the East. The last of the now dwindling Christian forces besieged and with great difficulty took Antioch, which the Mohammedans had got hold of a few years before. Here another Crusading leader made himself feudal lord, and there was a long delay and a bad quarrel between the Crusaders and the Emperor of Constantinople, who naturally wanted them to return to him what had been portions of his realm before Mohammedanism had grown up — while the Crusaders wanted to keep what they had conquered so that the revenues might become an income for each of them.

At last they got away from Antioch at the beginning of the open season of the third year after they had started — the last year of the eleventh century, 1099; they took all the towns along the coast as they marched; when they got on a level with Jerusalem they struck inland and stormed the city on the 15th of July of that year, killing all the Mohammedan garrison and establishing themselves firmly within the walls of the Holy City. They then organized their capture into a feudal kingdom, making one of their number titular King of the new realm of Jerusalem. They chose for that office a great noble of the country where the Teutonic and Gallic races meet in the north-east of France — Godfrey of Bouillon, a powerful Lord of the Marches. He had under him as nominal inferiors the great feudal lords who had carved out districts for themselves from Edessa southwards, and those who had built and established themselves in the great stone castles which still remain, among the finest ruins in the world.

By the time the Crusaders had accomplished their object and seized the Holy Places they had dwindled to a very small number of men. It is probable that the actual fighting men, as distinguished from servants, camp followers and the rest, present at the siege of Jerusalem, did not count much more than 15,000. And upon that force everything turned. Syria had not been thoroughly recovered, nor the Mohammedans finally thrust back; the seacoast was held with the support of a population still largely Christian, but the plain and the seacoast and Palestine up to the Jordan make only a narrow strip behind which and parallel to which comes a range of hills which in the middle of the country are great mountains — the Lebanon and the Anti-Lebanon. Behind that again the country turns into desert, and on the edge of the desert there is a string, of towns which are, as it were, the ports of the desert — that is, the points where the caravans arrive.

These "ports of the desert" have always been rendered very important by commerce, and their names go back well beyond the beginning of recorded history. A string of towns thus stretched along the edge of the desert begins from Aleppo in the north down as far as Petra, south of the Dead Sea. They were united by the great caravan route which reaches to North Arabia, and they were all predominantly Mohammedan by the time of the Crusading effort. The central one of these towns and the richest, the great market of Syria, is Damascus. If the first Crusaders had had enough men to take Damascus their effort would have been permanently successful. But their forces were insufficient for that, they could only barely hold the sea coast of Palestine up to the Jordan — and even so they held it only by the aid of immense fortified works.

There was a good deal of commerce with Europe, but not sufficient recruitment of forces, and the consequence was that the vast sea of Mohammedanism all around began to seep in and undermine the Christian position. The first sign of what was coming was the fall of Edessa (the capital of the north-eastern state of the Crusading federation, the state most exposed to attack), less than half a century after the first capture of Jerusalem.

It was the first serious set-back, and roused great

excitement in the Christian West. The Kings of France and England set out with great armies to re-establish the Crusading position, and this time they went for the strategic key of the whole country — Damascus. But they failed to take it: and when they and their men sailed back again the position of the Crusaders in Syria was as perilous as it had been before. They were guaranteed another lease of precarious security as long as the Mohammedan world was divided into rival bodies, but it was certain that if ever a leader should arise who could unify the Mohammedan power in his hands the little Christian garrisons were doomed.

And this is exactly what happened. Salah-ed-Din — whom we call Saladin — a soldier of genius, the son of a former Governor of Damascus, gradually acquired all power over the Mohammedan world of the Near East. He became master of Egypt, master of all the towns on the fringe of the desert, and when he marched to the attack with his united forces the remaining Christian body of Syria had no chance of victory. They made a fine rally, withdrawing every available man from their castle garrisons and forming a mobile force which attempted to relieve the siege of the castle of Tiberias on the Sea of Galilee. The Christian Army was approaching Tiberias and had got as far as the sloping mountain-side of Hattin, about a day's march away, when it was attacked by Saladin and destroyed.

The Great and Enduring Heresy of Mohammed

That disaster, which took place in the summer of 1187, was followed by the collapse of nearly the whole Christian military colony in Syria and the Holy Land. Saladin took town after town, save one or two points on the seacoast which were to remain in Christian hands more than another lifetime. But the kingdom of Jerusalem, the feudal Christian realm which had recovered and held the Holy Places, was gone. Jerusalem itself fell, of course, and its fall produced an enormous effect in Europe. All the great leaders, the King of England, Richard Plantagenet, the King of France and the Emperor, commanding jointly a large and first-rate army mainly German in recruitment, all set out to recover what had been lost. But they failed. They managed to get hold of one or two more points on the coast, but they never retook Jerusalem and never re-established the old Christian kingdom.

Thus ended a series of three mighty duels between Christendom and Islam. Islam had won.

Had the Crusaders' remaining force at the end of the first Crusading march been a little more numerous, had they taken Damascus and the string of towns on the fringe of the desert, the whole history of the world would have been changed. The world of Islam would have been cut in two, with the East unable to approach the West; probably we Europeans would have recovered North Africa and Egypt — we should certainly have

141

saved Constantinople — and Mohammedanism would only have survived as an Oriental religion thrust beyond the ancient boundaries of the Roman Empire. As it was Mohammedanism not only survived but grew stronger. It was indeed slowly thrust out of Spain and the eastern islands of the Mediterranean, but it maintained its hold on the whole of North Africa, Syria, Palestine, Asia Minor, and thence it went forward and conquered the Balkans and Greece, overran Hungary and twice threatened to overrun Germany and reach France again from the East, putting an end to our civilization. One of the reasons that the breakdown of Christendom at the Reformation took place was the fact that Mohammedan pressure against the German Emperor gave the German Princes and towns the opportunity to rebel and start Protestant Churches in their dominions.

Many expeditions followed against the Turk in one form or another; they were called Crusades, and the idea continued until the very end of the Middle Ages. But there was no recovery of Syria and no thrusting back of the Moslem.

Meanwhile the first Crusading march had brought so many new experiences to Western Europe that culture had developed very rapidly and produced the magnificent architecture and the high philosophy and social structure of the Middle Ages. That was the real fruit of the Crusades. They failed in their own field but they made modern Europe. Yet they made it at the expense of the old idea of Christian unity; with increasing material civilization, modern nations began to form, Christendom still held together, but it held together loosely. At last came the storm of the Reformation; Christendom broke up, the various nations and Princes claimed to be independent of any common control such as the moral position of the Papacy had insured, and we slid down that slope which was to end at last in the wholesale massacre of modern war — which may prove the destruction of our civilization. Napoleon Bonaparte very well said: *Every war in Europe is really a civil war.* It is profoundly true. Christian Europe is and should be by nature one; but it has forgotten its nature in forgetting its religion.

The last subject but one in our appreciation of the great Mohammedan attack upon the Catholic Church and the civilization she had produced, is the sudden last effort and subsequent rapid decline of Mohammedan political power just after it had reached its summit. The last subject of all in this connection, the one which I will treat next, is the very important and almost neglected question of whether Mohammedan power may not re-arise in the modern world.

If we recapitulate the fortunes of Islam after its triumph in beating back the Crusaders and restoring its dominion over the East and confirming its increasing grasp over half of what had once been a united Græco-Roman Christendom, Islam proceeded to develop two completely different and even contradictory fortunes: it was gradually losing its hold on Western Europe while it was increasing its hold over South-eastern Europe.

In Spain it had already been beaten back halfway from the Pyrenees to the Straits of Gibraltar before the Crusades were launched and it was destined in the next four to five centuries to lose every inch of ground which it had governed in the Iberian Peninsula: today called "Spain and Portugal." Continental Western Europe (and even the islands attached to it) was cleared of Mohammedan influence during the last centuries of the Middle Ages, the twelfth to fifteenth centuries.

This was because the Mohammedans of the West, that is, what was then called "Barbary," what is now French and Italian North Africa, were politically separated from the vast majority of the Mohammedan world which lay to the East.

Between the Barbary states (which we call today Tunis, Algiers and Morocco) and Egypt, the desert made a barrier difficult to cross. The West was less barren in former times than it is today, and the Italians are reviving its prosperity. But the vast stretches of sand and gravel, with very little water, always made this barrier between Egypt and the West a deterrent and an obstacle. Yet, more important than this barrier was the gradual disassociation between the Western Mohammedans of North Africa and the mass of Mohammedans to the East thereof. The religion indeed remained the same and the social habits and all the rest. Mohammedanism in North Africa remained one world with Mohammedanism in Syria, Asia and Egypt, just as the Christian civilization in the West of Europe remained for long one world with the Christian civilization of Central Europe and even of Eastern Europe. But distance and the fact that the Eastern Mohammedans never sufficiently came to their help made the Western Mohammedans of North Africa and of Spain feel themselves something separate politically from their Eastern brethren.

To this we must add the factor of distance and its effect on sea power in those days and in those waters. The Mediterranean is much more than two thousand miles long; the only period of the year in which any effective fighting could be done on its waters under mediaeval conditions was the late spring, summer and early autumn and it is precisely in those five months of the year, when alone men could use the Mediterranean for great expeditions, that offensive military operations were handicapped by long calms. It is true these were met by the use of many-oared galleys so as to make fleets as little dependent on wind as possible, but still, distances of that kind did make unity of action difficult.

Therefore, the Mohammedans of North Africa not being supported at sea by the wealth and numbers of their brethren from the ports of Asia Minor and of Syria and the mouths of the Nile, gradually lost control of maritime communications. They lost, therefore, the Western islands, Sicily and Corsica and Sardinia, the Balearics and even Malta at the very moment when they were triumphantly capturing the Eastern islands in the Ægean Sea. The only form of sea power remaining to the Mohammedan in the West was the active piracy of the Algerian sailors operating from the lagoon of Tunis and the half-sheltered bay of Algiers. (The word "Algiers" comes from the Arabic word for "islands." There was no proper harbour before the French conquest of a hundred years ago, but there was a roadstead partially sheltered by a string of rocks and islets.) These pirates remained a peril right on until the seventeenth century. It is interesting to notice, for instance, that the Mohammedan call to prayer was heard on the coasts of Southern Ireland within the lifetime of Oliver Cromwell, for the Algerian pirates darted about everywhere, not only in the Western

Mediterranean but along the coasts of the Atlantic, from the Straits of Gibraltar to the English Channel. They were no longer capable of conquest, but they could loot and take prisoners whom they held to ransom.

While this beating back of the Mohammedan into Africa was going on to the Western side of Europe, exactly the opposite was happening on the *Eastern* side. After the Crusades had failed Mohammedans made themselves secure in Asia Minor and began that long hammering at Constantinople which finally succeeded.

Constantinople was by far the richest and greatest capital of the Ancient World; it was the old centre of Greek and Roman civilization and even when it had lost all direct political power over Italy, and still more over France, it continued to be revered as the mighty monument of the Roman past. The Emperor of Constantinople was the direct heir of the Caesars. On the military side this very strong city supported by great masses of tribute and by a closely knit, well disciplined army, was the bulwark of Christendom. So long as Constantinople stood as a Christian city and Mass was still said in St. Sophia, the doors of Europe were locked against Islam. It fell in the same generation that saw the expulsion of the last Mohammedan Government from Southern Spain. Men who in their maturity marched into Granada with the victorious armies of Isabella the Catholic could remember how, in early childhood, they had heard the awful news that Constantinople itself had fallen to the enemies of the Church.

The fall of Constantinople at the end of the Middle Ages (1453) was only the beginning of further Mohammedan advances. Islam swept all over the Balkans; it took all the Eastern Mediterranean islands, Crete and Rhodes and the rest; it completely occupied Greece; it began pushing up the Danube valley and northwards into the great plains; it destroyed the ancient kingdom of Hungary in the fatal battle of Mohacs and at last, in the first third of the sixteenth century, just at the moment when the storm of the Reformation had broken out, Islam threatened Europe close at hand, bringing pressure upon the heart of the Empire, at Vienna.

It is not generally appreciated how the success of Luther's religious revolution against Catholicism in Germany was due to the way in which Mohammedan pressure from the East was paralysing the central authority of the German Emperors. They had to compromise with the leaders of the religious revolution and try to patch up a sort of awkward peace between the irreconcilable claims of Catholic authority and Protestant religious theory in order to meet the enemy at their gates; the enemy which had already overthrown Hungary and might well overthrow all Southern Germany and perhaps reach the Rhine. If Islam had succeeded in doing this during the chaos of violent civil dissension among the Germans, due to the launching of the Reformation, our civilization would have been as effectively destroyed as it would have been if the first rush of the Mohammedans through Spain had not been checked and beaten back eight centuries earlier in the middle of France.

This violent Mohammedan pressure on Christendom from the East made a bid for success by sea as well as by land. The last great wave of Mongol soldiery, the last great Turkish organization working now from the conquered capital of Constantinople, proposed to cross the Adriatic, to attack Italy by sea and ultimately to recover all that had been lost in the Western Mediterranean.

There was one critical moment when it looked as though the scheme would succeed. A huge Mohammedan armada fought at the mouth of the Gulf of Corinth against the Christian fleet at Lepanto. The Christians won that naval action and the Western Mediterranean was saved. But it was a very close thing, and the name of Lepanto should remain in the minds of all men with a sense of history as one of the half dozen great names in the history of the Christian world. It has been a worthy theme for the finest battle poem of our time, " The Ballad of Lepanto," by the late Mr. Gilbert Chesterton.

Today we are accustomed to think of the Mohammedan world as something backward and stagnant, in all material affairs at least. We cannot imagine a great Mohammedan fleet made up of modern ironclads and submarines, or a great modern Mohammedan army fully equipped with modern artillery, flying power and the rest. But not so very long ago, *less than a hundred years before the Declaration of Independence*, the Mohammedan Government centred at Constantinople had better artillery and better army equipment of every kind than had we Christians in the West. The last effort they made to destroy Christendom was contemporary with the end of the reign of Charles II in England and of his brother James and of the usurper William III. It failed during the last years of the seventeenth century, only just over two hundred years ago. Vienna, as we saw, was almost taken and only saved by the Christian army under the command of the King of Poland on a date that ought to be among the most famous in history — September 11th, 1683. But the peril remained, Islam was still immensely powerful within a few marches of Austria and it was not until the great victory of Prince Eugene at Zenta in 1697 and the capture of Belgrade that the tide really turned — and by that time we were at the end of the seventeenth century.

It should be fully grasped that the generation of Dean Swift, the men who saw the court of Louis XIV in old age, the men who saw the Hanoverians brought in as puppet Kings for England by the dominating English wealthy class, the men who saw the apparent extinction of Irish freedom after the failure of James II's campaign at the Boyne and the later surrender of Limerick, all that lifetime which overlapped between the end of the seventeenth and the beginning of the eighteenth century, was dominated by a vivid memory of a Mohammedan threat which had very nearly made good and which apparently might in the near future be repeated. The Europeans of that time thought of Mohammedanism as we think of Bolshevism or as white men in Asia think of Japanese power today.

What happened was something quite unexpected; the Mohammedan power began to break down on the material side. The Mohammedans lost the power of competing successfully with the Christians in the making of those instruments whereby dominion is assured; armament, methods of communication and all the rest of it. Not only did they not advance, they went back. Their artillery became much worse than ours. While our use of the sea vastly increased, theirs sank away till they had no first-class ships with which to fight naval battles.

The eighteenth century is a story of their gradual losing of the race against the European in material things.

When that vast revolution in human affairs introduced by the invention of modern machinery began in England and spread slowly throughout Europe, the Mohammedan world proved itself quite incapable of taking advantage thereof. During the Napoleonic wars, although supported by England, Islam failed entirely to meet the French armies of Egypt; its last effort resulted in complete defeat (the land battle of the Nile).

All during the nineteenth century the process continued. As a result, Mohammedan North Africa was gradually subjected to European control; the last independent piece to go being Morocco. Egypt fell under the control of England. Long before that Greece had been liberated, and the Balkan States. Half a lifetime ago it was taken for granted everywhere that the last remnants of Mohammedan power in Europe would disappear. England bolstered it up and did save Constantinople from being taken by the Russians in 1877-78, but it seemed only a question of a few years before the Turks would be wiped out for good. Everyone was waiting for the end of Islam, on this side of the Bosphorus at least; while in Syria, Asia Minor and Mesopotamia it was losing all political and military vigour. After the Great War, what was left of Mohammedan power, even in Hither Asia, let alone in Constantinople, was only saved by the violent quarrels between the Allies.

Even Syria and Palestine were divided between France and England. Mesopotamia fell under the control of England and no menace of Islamic power remained, though it was still entrenched in Asia Minor and kept a sort of precarious hold on the thoroughly decayed city of Constantinople alone. The Mediterranean was gone; every inch of European territory was gone; all full control over African territory was gone; and the great duel between Islam and Christendom seemed at last to have been decided in our own day.

To what was due this collapse? I have never seen an answer to that question. There was no moral distintegration from within, there was no intellectual breakdown; you will find the Egyptian or Syrian student today, if you talk to him on any philosophical or scientific subject which he has studied, to be the equal of any European. If Islam has no physical science now applied to any of its problems, in arms and communications, it has apparently ceased to be part of our world and fallen definitely below it. Of every dozen Mohammedans in the world today, eleven are actually or virtually subjects of an Occidental power. It would seem, I repeat, as though the great duel was now decided.

But can we be certain it is so decided? I doubt it very much. It has always seemed to me possible, and even probable, that there would be a resurrection of Islam and that our sons or our grandsons would see the renewal of that tremendous struggle between the Christian culture and what has been for more than a thousand years its greatest opponent.

Why this conviction should have arisen in the minds of certain observers and travellers, such as myself, I will now consider. It is indeed a vital question, "May not Islam rise again?"

In a sense the question is already answered because Islam has never departed. It still commands the fixed loyalty and unquestioning adhesion of all the millions between the Atlantic and the Indus and further afield throughout scattered communities of further Asia. But I ask the question in the sense "Will not perhaps the temporal power of Islam return and with it the menace of an armed Mohammedan world which will shake off the domination of Europeans — still nominally Christian — and reappear again as the prime enemy of our civilization?" The future always comes as a surprise but political wisdom consists in attempting at least some partial judgment of what that surprise may be.

And for my part I cannot but believe that a main unexpected thing of the future is the return of Islam. Since religion is at the root of all political movements and changes and since we have here a very great religion physically paralysed but morally intensely alive, we are in the presence of an unstable equilibrium which cannot remain permanently unstable. Let us then examine the position.

I have said throughout these pages that the particular quality of Mohammedanism, regarded as a heresy, was its vitality. Alone of all the great heresies Mohammedanism struck permanent roots, developing a life of its own, and became at last something like a new religion. So true is this that today very few men, even among those who are highly instructed in history, recall the truth that Mohammedanism was essentially in its origins *not* a new religion, but a *heresy*.

Like all heresies, Mohammedanism lived by the Catholic truths which it had retained. Its insistence on personal immortality, on the Unity and Infinite Majesty of God, on His Justice and Mercy, its insistence on the equality of human souls in the sight of their Creator — these are its strength.

But it has survived for other reasons than these; all the other great heresies had their truths as well as their falsehoods and vagaries, yet they have died one after the other. The Catholic Church has seen them pass, and though their evil consequences are still with us the heresies themselves are dead.

The strength of Calvinism was the truth on which it insisted, the Omnipotence of God, the dependence and insufficiency of man; but its error, which was the negation of free-will, also killed it. For men could not permanently accept so monstrous a denial of common sense and common experience. Arianism lived by the truth that was in it, to wit, the fact that the reason could not directly reconcile the opposite aspects of a great mystery — that of the Incarnation. But Arianism died because it added to this truth a falsehood, to wit, that the apparent contradiction could be solved by denying the full Divinity of Our Lord.

And so on with the other heresies. But Mohammedanism, though it also contained errors side by side with those great truths, flourished continually, *and as a body of doctrine is flourishing still*, though thirteen hundred years have passed since its first great victories in Syria. The causes of this vitality are very difficult to explore, and perhaps cannot be reached. For myself I should ascribe it in some part to the fact that Mohammedanism being a thing from outside, a heresy that did not arise within the body of the Christian community but beyond its frontiers, has always possessed a reservoir of men, newcomers pouring in to revivify its energies. But that cannot be a full explanation; perhaps Mohammedanism would have died but for the successive waves of recruitment from the desert and from Asia; perhaps it would have died if the Caliphate at Baghdad had been left entirely to itself, and if the Moors in the West had not been able to draw upon continual recruitment from the South.

Whatever the cause be, Mohammedanism has survived, and vigorously survived. Missionary effort has had no appreciable effect upon it. It still converts pagan savages wholesale. It even attracts from time to time some European eccentric, who joins its body. *But the Mohammedan never becomes a Catholic.* No fragment of Islam ever abandons its sacred book, its code of morals, its organized system of prayer, its simple doctrine.

In view of this, anyone with a knowledge of history is bound to ask himself whether we shall not see in the future a revival of Mohammedan political power, and the renewal of the old pressure of Islam upon Christendom.

We have seen how the material political power of Islam declined very rapidly during the eighteenth and nineteenth centuries. We have just followed the story of that decline. When Suleiman the Magnificent was besieging Vienna he had better artillery, better energies and better everything than his opponents; Islam was

still in the field the material superior of Christendom
— at least it was the superior in fighting power and
fighting instruments. That was within a very few years
of the opening of the eighteenth century. Then came
the inexplicable decline. The religion did not decay, but
its political power and with that its material power
declined astonishingly, and in the particular business
of arms it declined most of all. When Dr. Johnson's
father, the bookseller, was setting up in business at
Lichfield, the Grand Turk was still dreaded as a
potential conqueror of Europe; before Dr. Johnson was
dead no Turkish fleet or army could trouble the West.
Not a lifetime later, the Mohammedan in North Africa
had fallen subject to the French; and those who were
then young men lived to see nearly all Mohammedan
territory, except for a decaying fragment ruled from
Constantinople, firmly subdued by the French and
British Governments.

These things being so, the recrudescence of Islam,
the possibility of that terror under which we lived for
centuries reappearing, and of our civilization again
fighting for its life against what was its chief enemy for
a thousand years, seems fantastic. Who in the
Mohammedan world today can manufacture and
maintain the complicated instruments of modern war?
Where is the political machinery whereby the religion

of Islam can play an equal part in the modern world?

I say the suggestion that Islam may re-arise sounds fantastic — but this is only because men are always powerfully affected by the immediate past: — one might say that they are blinded by it.

Cultures spring from religions; ultimately the vital force which maintains any culture is its philosophy, its attitude towards the universe; the decay of a religion involves the decay of the culture corresponding to it — we see that most clearly in the breakdown of Christendom today. The bad work begun at the Reformation is bearing its final fruit in the dissolution of our ancestral doctrines — the very structure of our society is dissolving.

In place of the old Christian enthusiasms of Europe there came, for a time, the enthusiasm for nationality, the religion of patriotism. But self-worship is not enough, and the forces which are making for the destruction of our culture, notably the Jewish Communist propaganda from Moscow*, have a likelier future before them than our old-fashioned patriotisms.

In Islam there has been no such dissolution of ancestral doctrine — or, at any rate, nothing corresponding to the universal break-up of religion in Europe. The whole spiritual strength of Islam is still present in the masses of Syria and Anatolia, of the East

Asian mountains, of Arabia, Egypt and North Africa.

The final fruit of this tenacity, the second period of Islamic power, may be delayed: — but I doubt whether it can be permanently postponed.

There is nothing in the Mohammedan civilization itself which is hostile to the development of scientific knowledge or of mechanical aptitude. I have seen some good artillery work in the hands of Mohammedan students of that arm; I have seen some of the best driving and maintenance of mechanical road transport conducted by Mohammedans. There is nothing inherent to Mohammedanism to make it incapable of modern science and modern war. Indeed the matter is not worth discussing. It should be self-evident to anyone who has seen the Mohammedan culture at work. That culture happens to have fallen back in material applications; there is no reason whatever why it should not learn its new lesson and become our equal in all those temporal things which now *alone* give us our superiority over it — whereas in *Faith* we have fallen inferior to it.

People who question this may be misled by a number of false suggestions dating from the immediate past. For instance; it was a common saying during the nineteenth century that Mohammedanism had lost its political power through its doctrine of fatalism. But that doctrine was in full vigour when the Mohammedan

power was at its height. For that matter Mohammedanism is no more fatalist than Calvinism; the two
heresies resemble each other exactly in their exaggerated
insistence upon the immutability of divine decrees.

There was another more intelligent suggestion
made in the nineteenth century, which was this: — that
the decline of Islam had proceeded from its fatal habit
of perpetual civil division; the splitting up and
changeability of political authority among the
Mohammedans. But that weakness of theirs was
present from the beginning; it is inherent in the very
nature of the Arabian temperament from which they
started. Over and over again this individualism of
theirs, this " fissiparous " tendency of theirs, has gravely
weakened them; yet over and over again they have
suddenly united under a leader and accomplished the
greatest things.

Now it is probable enough that on these lines —
unity under a leader — the return of Islam may arrive.
There is no leader as yet, but enthusiasm might bring
one and there are signs enough in the political heavens
today of what we may have to expect from the revolt of
Islam at some future date — perhaps not far distant.

After the Great War the Turkish power was suddenly
restored by one such man. Another such man in
Arabia, with equal suddenness, affirmed himself and
destroyed all the plans laid for the incorporation of

that part of the Mohammedan world into the English sphere. Syria, which is the connecting link, the hinge and the pivot of the whole Mohammedan world, is, upon the map, and superficially, divided between an English and a French mandate; but the two Powers intrigue one against the other and are equally detested by their Mohammedan subjects, who are only kept down precariously by force. There has been bloodshed under the French mandate more than once and it will be renewed*; while under the English mandate the forcing of an alien Jewish colony upon Palestine has raised the animosity of the native Arab population to white heat. Meanwhile a ubiquitous underground Bolshevist propaganda is working throughout Syria and North Africa continually, against the domination of Europeans over the original Mohammedan population.

Lastly there is this further point to which attention should be paid:—the attachment (such as it is) of the Mohammedan world in India to English rule is founded mainly upon the gulf between the Mohammedan and the Hindu religions. Every step towards a larger political independence for either party strengthens the Mohammedan desire for renewed power. The Indian Mohammedan will more and more tend to say: "If I am to look after myself and not to be favoured as I have been in the past by the alien European master in India — which I once ruled — I will rely upon the revival of Islam." For all these reasons (and many more might be added) men of foresight may justly apprehend, or at any rate expect, the return of Islam.

It would seem as though the Great Heresies were granted an effect proportionate to the lateness of their appearance in the story of Christendom. The earlier heresies on the Incarnation, when they died out, left no enduring relic of their presence. Arianism was revived for a moment in the general chaos of the Reformation. Sundry scholars, including Milton in England and presumably Bruno in Italy and a whole group of Frenchmen put forward doctrines in the sixteenth and seventeenth centuries which attempted to reconcile a modified materialism and a denial of the Trinity with some part of Christian religion. Milton's effort was particularly noticeable. English official history has, of course, suppressed it as much as possible, by the usual method of scamping all emphasis upon it. The English historians do not deny Milton's materialism; quite recently several English writers on Milton have discoursed at length on his refusal of full divinity to Our Lord. But this effort at suppression will break down, for one cannot forever hide a thing so important as Milton's attack, not only on the Incarnation, but on the Creation, and on the omnipotence of Almighty God.

But of that I will speak later when we come to the Protestant movement. It remains generally true that the earlier heresies not only died out but left no enduring memorial of their action on European society.

But Mohammedanism coming as much later than Arianism as Arianism was later than the Apostles has left a profound effect on the political structure of Europe and upon language: even to some extent on science.

Politically, it destroyed the independence of the Eastern Empire and though various fragments have, some of them, revived in maimed fashion, the glory and unity of Byzantine rule disappeared forever under the attacks of Islam. The Russian Tsardom, oddly enough, took over a maimed inheritance from Byzantium, but it was a very poor reflection of the old Greek splendour. The truth is that Islam permanently wounded the east of our civilization in such fashion that barbarism partly returned.

* Written in March, 1936.

Other titles from
ROGER A. McCAFFREY PUBLISHING

The Real Problems of Real People:
Solutions for Christians
Harry Emerson Fosdick, $19.95

Psychological Seduction
William Kilpatrick, $19.95

Guidance in Spiritual Direction
Charles Hugo Doyle, $25.95

The Emperor's New Clothes
William Kilpatrick, $19.95

The Montessori Method
Maria Montessori, $24.80

Preaching Well
William Duffey, $25.75

Loyola and the Educational System of the Jesuits
Thomas Hughes, $27.95

The Story of Therese Neumann
Albert Schimberg, $19.95